BIBLICAL SITES
IN TURKEY

BIBLICAL SITES
IN TURKEY

Everett C. Blake
&
Anna G. Edmonds

ISBN 975-8176-26-9

BIBLICAL SITES IN TURKEY
Authors: Everett C. Blake, Anna G. Edmonds
Yayım Hakkı/Copyright © 1997, SEV Matbaacılık ve Yayıncılık A.Ş.
First Edition/Birinci Basım: 1977
Eighth Edition/Sekizinci Basım: 1997
Baskı/Printing: Uycan Yayınları San. ve Tic. A.Ş.
Kapak Fotoğrafı/ Cover Photo: Ersin Alok
Haritalar/Maps: Cezibe Hoşgören

Sev Matbaacılık ve Yayıncılık A.Ş.
Merkez: Beyazgül Sk. 96/1 Arnavutköy/Beşiktaş
İrtibat : Rızapaşa Yokuşu No: 50 Mercan 34450 İstanbul

Tel: 0.212.522 14 98

CONTENTS

PAGE

PREFACES IX
TIME CHART XIII
MAPS following page XIV

CHAPTER I: TURKISH BACKGROUNDS 1

Geography 1; Government 2; Monetary Unit 2; Language 2: Religion 3; Atatürk Reforms 4; History 5

CHAPTER II: ANATOLIA IN THE TIME OF THE OLD TESTAMENT 9

Introduction 9; The Land 10; The Peoples 11; The Names 12; Descendents of Noah 13; Shem's Family: the Semites 15; Asshur 16; Lud 16; Arphaxad 17; Aram 17; Ham's Family: the Hamites 18; Mizraim — the Lydians 18; — the Caphtorites 19; Canaan — Heth 19; — the Hivites (Hurrians) 20; Japheth's Family: the Japhethites 21; Gomer 21; — Ashkenaz 22; — Riphath 22; — Togarmah 22; Magog 23; Madai 23; Javan 23; — Tarshish 24; Tubal 24; Meshech 25; Tiras 25; References Outside the Table of Nations 26; Ararat 26; Minni 27; Sepharad 27; Coa 28

CHAPTER III: OLD TESTAMENT LOCATIONS 29

Cudi Dağı, Karabur, Zincirli 30; Harran 31; Edessa 41; Carchemish 41; Tubal 42; Boğazkale, Yazılı Kaya, Alaca Höyük 43; Kanesh 43; Gordium 44; Togarmah 46; Mt. Ararat 46; Van, Toprakkale 48; Sepharad, Sardis 49; Tigris and Euphrates 49; Eden 51

CHAPTER IV: ANATOLIA IN THE TIME OF THE NEW TESTAMENT 53

Political Divisions 53; Southern Coast: Cilicia 54; Pamphylia 54; Lycia 54; Interior: Commagene 55; Cappadocia 55; Galatia 56; Isauria — Lycaonia 56; Pisidia 56; Phrygia 57; Aegean Coast: Caria 57; Asia 57; Lydia 58; Mysia 58; Troas 58; Black Sea: Bithynia 59;

Paphlagonia 59; Pontus 59; Europe: Thrace 59; Pagan
Religions: Cybele 61; Mithra 61; Artemis 62; Aphrodite
62; Apollo 62; Athena 63; Poseidon 63; Pan 63;
Dionysus 63; Zeus 63; Judaism 64; Education, Culture
65; The Union of East and West 66

CHAPTER V: TURKEY'S SOUTHERN COAST   69
Antioch 69; Seleucia 72; Tarsus 73; Silifke 76

CHAPTER VI: CENTRAL TURKEY   77

Caesarea Mazaca 77; Ürgüp, Göreme 78; Derinkuyu,
Kaymaklı 79; Tavium 79; Ancyra 80; Pessinus 81;
Antioch of Pisidia 81; İconium 83; Lystra 85; Derbe 86

CHAPTER VII: THE GULF OF ATTALIA   89
Attalia 89; Perga 90; Myra 92; Patara 93

CHAPTER VIII: TURKEY'S AEGEAN AND MARMARA
     AREAS   95

Cnidus 95; Miletus 96; Trogillium 99; Colossae 99;
Hierapolis 101; Adramyttium 102; Assos 102; Alexandria Troas 103; Nicaea 113; Byzantium 114

CHAPTER IX: THE SEVEN CHURCHES OF REVELATION   117

Ephesus 119; Smyrna 124; Pergamum 128; Thyatira
131; Sardis 133; Philadelphia 137; Laodicea 139

CONCLUSION   143
APPENDIX I: PAUL'S JOURNEYS   145
APPENDIX II: COMPARATIVE LIST OF PLACE NAMES   149
APPENDIX III: SUGGESTED TOURS   155
BIBLIOGRAPHY   161
LIST OF ILLUSTRATIONS   167
INDEX   169

To our families

with whom we have shared

the beauty and hospitality of Turkey,

the unspoiled "Holy Land."

Preface to the First Edition

Turkey, as part of the land of the Near East, is an important corner of the stage on which the history of Western man has been played. Here in the Near East are some of the earliest records of people's struggles for dominion over all the earth. It is in this area that the three great monotheistic religions, Judaism, Christianity, and Islam, have developed. In Anatolia early Christianity took shape and spread so that by 393 A.D. it had become the state religion of the Roman Empire.

Thus a journey through this part of the world often has something of the quality of a pilgrimage, both a physical and a spiritual search for the origins and realities of one's faith. While the modern travelers will see land and water and vegetation when they look at the remains of historical sites, still they should know that it is with these resources that the generations before have shaped their lives and influenced the development of our history, just as the people living here today are doing. One can gain understanding of history and personal inspiration in the search by seeing the physical locations and observing the customs that are reminiscent of biblical records, but the lasting value will always remain in the way one's life is changed by it. This is the pilgrimage.

The purpose of this book is to give a brief background of the country of Turkey from the point of view of foreigners who have lived here many years, to note biblical references to places here, and to give some information concerning their historical and present interest. This is not intended to be a general guidebook since several good ones already exist, but rather a supplement for those interested particularly in the physical environment of people in the Bible and in the early Christian church.

Some of the biblical references are given in the body of the material; more are listed at the beginning of the chapters. The quotations are taken from the *New English Bible,* second edition (c. 1970) by permission of Oxford and Cambridge University Presses. The biblical or historical place name is given first, then the present Turkish name if there is an equivalent. Those using a current Turkish road map should refer to Appendix 2 for cross-referencing on names.

Thanks are due to a number of people. Any book on this subject depends first on the work of countless biblical scholars through the centuries. They are acknowledged, although only formally, in the bibliography at the end. More immediately, Mr. Robert Avery, senior editor of Redhouse Press, first edited the material. Without his work the final task would have been much more difficult. The Reverend Gregory Seeber, minister of the Union Church of Istanbul, also made a number of useful comments. Dr. Henri Metzger, director of the French Archeological Institute in Istanbul, and his wife gave incalculable help. Dr. Metzger read the entire manuscript as did Dr. U. Bahadır Alkım, archeologist and professor at the University of Istanbul. Dr. Alkım also gave unstintingly of his time and help. Many, many people — museum officals including Dr. Necati Dolunay, director of the Istanbul Archeological Museums, Mr. İlhan Temizsöy, director of the Karaman Museum, Mr. Osman Özbek of that same museum, various guides, students, farmers, and children — throughout Turkey and over the years have contributed to our knowledge of the country and our appreciation of its riches. The authors' families are also to be thanked for their support, advice, and patience.
It is the hope of the authors and of Redhouse Press that this guide will help make the journey among these sites both pleasurable and of lasting value.

September 1977   E.C.B., A.G.E.

Preface to the Second Edition

This second edition has been revised in the light of comments from our readers and our increased information about many of the sites. It has been our privilege to visit a number of the places again since the first edition was published. What we have gained from these visits we have included in the text.

We also were helped by Mrs. Anne Metzger who prepared the French translation of this book, *Sites Bibliques de Turquie* (published in 1978), by Mrs. Suna Asımgil who has worked on the Turkish edition (yet to be published), and again by the Reverend Gregory Seeber.

The spelling of proper names in this book follows where possible that used in the *New English Bible.* Otherwise the common American or Turkish spellings are used. An attempt has been made to give both the biblical and the Turkish place names. There is a comparative list of these in Appendix 2.

We hope this new edition will enjoy the success accorded the earlier ones, and that it, too, will be a useful guide.

January 1982   E.C.B., A.G.E.

8500 B.C.   Neolithic Period. Çatal Höyük 6800-5700.

5000   Chalcolithic Period.

4000   Bronze Age; Cultivation of wheat, barley, grapes, figs, olives, onions, beans, peas, probably rye.

3500   Sumerians. Explosion of Thera 3,370.

3000   Upper and Lower Egypt united 3200. Cuneiform first written language in Mesopotamia c. 3000. Helladic culture on mainland Greece, Cyladic on islands. Old Kingdom in Egypt 2686-2181; Great Pyramid of Khufu 2600. King Gilgamish of Erech 2650. Classical Sumerian Period c. 2800-2360. Kish main Sumerian city.

2500   Middle Kingdom of Egypt 2133 - 1786, XI Dynasty c. 2160. Akkadian Dynasty 2360-2180. Sargon the Great 2325. Gilgamish Epic current in Mesopotamia. Ur-Nammu founded last Sumerian dynasty with capital in Ur, promulgated law code 2100.

2000   Hatti people in Anatolia. Hebrews nomadic shepherds in Canaan 2000-1700; Abraham 2000-1900 (? or 1750). Mycenaeans in Greece 2000-1700. XII Dynasty in Egypt: Amenhemet I 1991-1962, Senusret I 1971-1928. Elamites destroyed Ur.

1950

1900   Assyrian traders in Anatolia 1900-1700. Middle Bronze Age. First Indo-European migration from Caucasus into Cappadocia of Hittites, Hurrians, Hivites.

1850   Hittite power begins. Assyrian control in Upper Mesopotamia.

1800   King Anittas of Kanesh.

1750   Old Hittite Kingdom, Labarnas I c. 1750. Hammurabi king in Babylon 1704-1662 (? 1750-1708). Joseph (?). Hyksos kings in Egypt c. 1720 introduce horse-drawn chariots.

1700   Minoan culture 1700-1500.

1650   Hattusilis I 1650-1621 and Mursilis I 1620-1590 Hittite kings.

1600   New Kingdom dynasty in Egypt, Ahmose I 1580-1550. Babylonian Empire destroyed by Hittites.

1550   Hittite Empire Harran important city. Amenophis I 1550-1528, Tuthmosis I 1528-1510.

1500   Mitanni Kingdom of Hurrians. Battle of Megiddo 1468. Linear B script on Crete. Tuthmosis III 1490-1436 conquered Syria. King Telipinus, Hittite lawgiver.

1450   Amarna Age in Egypt, Amenophis III 1405-1367.

1400   Suppiluliumas in Anatolia 1375-1335 (? 1380-1346). Mycenaeans gained superiority in Greece, Knossus collapsed. Amenophis Ikhnaton IV 1367-1350; Nefertiti.

1350   Mitanni overthrown. Ugarit. Tut-ankh-Amon 1347-1339; Horemheb 1335-1308 (?).

1300   Hurri overthrown. Moses, Exodus. Ramses II 1290-1224 completed temples at Karnak. Battle of Qadesh 1285. Egypto-Hittite treaty 1269.

1250   Phoenicians flourishing. Hebrews entered Canaan; fall of Jericho 1250 (?). Joshua.

1200   Trojan Wars. Phrygian invasion 1190. Rule of Judges. Sea Peoples c. 1175. Ramses III 1195-1164.

1150   Tiglath-pileser I 1115.1077. Nebuchadrezzar I 1124 1103.

1100   Domestication and increasing use of camels.

1050   Neo-Hittite Kingdom. Saul 1020-1004; David 1010-955.

1000   Solomon 955-935 (? 965-925). Latin tribes began to settle. Phoenicians a sea power 1000-774.

950   Israel: Jeroboam 931-910; Judah : Rehoboam 931-915. Assyrian Empire controlled Mesopotamia. 910-606.

900   Etruscans from Lydia settled Italy, became maritime power.

850   Homeric Greece 850-600. Hesiod. Semiramis 810-806. King Ispuinis 830-810.

800   Northern Kingdom in Palestine. Olympic Games began 776. Carthage founded by Phoenicians. Rome founded by Romulus and Remus 753.

750   Sardur III (?) Urartu king. Midas 725-675. Amos, Hosea, Micah, Isaiah. Hezekiah 715-686. Israelites exiled. Sparta powerful 737-630. Tiglath-pileser III (also called Pul) 745-727 king of Assyria subdued Aramaeans, conquered Urartu,

controlled Syria. Sargon II 720-705 completed conquest of Israel. Sennacherib 704-681 built palace at Nineveh. Ambaris of Tabal. Rusa I of Urartu fought with Merodach-baladan of Babylon against Sargon II.

700 Gyges of Lydia. Byzantium founded by Megara 660. Ashurbanipal 668-631; height of Assyrian power. Sack of Babylon 689. Sack of Tarsus by Sennacherib 696.

650 Battle of Carchemish 605 ended Assyrian Empire. Necho 610-595 defeated by Nebuchadrezzar II 605-562 at Carchemish. Hanging gardens, Tower of Babel. Josiah 632-608. Chaldean Empire 625-539. Nineveh destroyed 612. Battle of Megiddo 608. Jeremiah 626.

600 Median Empire. Sack of Smyrna by Lydians 595. Urartu overthrown 585. Solar eclipse 28 May 585. Alyattes king of Lydia. Croesus 560-546 defeated by Cyrus the Great. Jerusalem captured 597, temple of Solomon destroyed March 15-16, again in 587. Ezekiel one of captives sent to Mesopotamia 598. Solon introduced constitutional, social reforms in Athens 594. First Roman census 566. Cyrus 559-530 conquered Babylon, returned Hebrews to Jerusalem 538.

550 Temple of Artemis in Ephesus. Persians conquered Egypt 525-404. Darius I 521-485 unified Persian power. Achaeminian Age. Founding of Roman Republic 509.

500 Classical Greek civilization, Psalms written (?). Persian War 499-449, Battle of Marathon 490. Age of Pericles 457-429. Roman law codified 451. Xerxes I 485-465. Heroditus c. 490-425.

450 Parthenon built 447-432. Peloponnesian War 431-404; Athens destroyed 430.

400 Sparta leading power 404-371. Socrates condemned to death 399. Rome sacked by Gauls 390. Mausoleum at Halicarnassus 352.

350 Hellenistic Period 323-31 B.C. Seleucis I 305-281. Plato founded Academy 387; Aristotle founded Lyceum 335. Philip of Macedon 359-336; Alexander 336-323. Ptolomy Dynasty in Egypt 323 B.C. — 30 A.D.

300 Antiochus I 281-261. Rome became major power. Pyrrus fought Romans 282-272. First Punic War 264-241. Alexandria intellectual center of Hellenistic world to 50 B.C.

250 Second Punic War 218-201. Attalus I moved Magna Mater Magnum Idaea from Pessinus to Rome 204. Parthian Empire 250 B.C. — 226 A.D.

200   Syrian War 192-189; Rome conquered Asia Minor. Maccabean Revolt 167.

150   Pergamum given to Rome by Attalus III 133. Book of Isaiah. Third Punic War, Carthage destroyed 149-146. Formation of Roman Province of Asia 129.

100   "Asian Vespers" 88. Mithradates VI Eupator d. 63. Third Mithradatic War 74-63 led to Roman conquests in Near East Pompey against pirates 67. Seleucid dynasty end 63. Sparticus led slave revolt 73-71. First Triumvirate of Julius Caesar, Pompey, Marcus Licinius Crassus 60-53.

50   Cicero governor Cilicia 51-50. Roman rule of Palestine began 37. Caesar ruled Rome 46-44. Second Triumvirate of Mark Anthony, Lepidus, Octavian 43-21. Vergil. Horace. Roman Empire established 27. Pax Romana 14 B.C. — 192 A.D. Octavian defeated Anthony and Cleopatra 31. Egypt annexed to Rome 30. Jesus born.

1 A.D.   John the Baptist preaching c. 28, Jesus crucified c. 30. Paul preaching 42-60 James martyred 44. Josephus 37-100.

50   Paul and Peter martyred in Rome. Nero 54. Rome burned 64. Jews revolted against Rome 66. Jerusalem destroyed Vesuvius erupted 79. Domitian 81. Trajan 98.

100   Pliny governor of Bithynia 111-112. Ignatius martyred 115 (?). Hadrian 117.

150   Polycarp martyred 155. Bar Kokba led unsuccessful Jewish revolt 132-135; Jews barred from Jerusalem. Marcus Aurelius 160-180.

200   Diocletian 284. Constantine the Great 306. Ecumenical Councils: First in Nicaea 325, Second in Constantinople 381, Third in Ephesus 431, Fourth in Chalcedon 451, Fifth in Constantinople 553, Sixth in Constantinople 680-681, Seventh in Nicaea 787. Edict of Milan 313. Constantinople capital of Roman Empire 330. St. Sophia completed 537. Muhammed born 570, Hegira 622.

Van Castle

Ahtamar

Trabzon: Church of St. Sophia

Sumela: Monastery of the Virgin

CHAPTER I
TURKISH BACKGROUNDS

GEOGRAPHY

Modern Turkey is a country of 780,576 square kilometers, somewhat larger than the state of Texas or France and Great Britain combined. It is bordered by the Mediterranean, Aegean, and Black Seas, by Greece, Bulgaria, Georgia, Armenia, Nahcıvan, Iran, Iraq, and Syria. About three percent of the country is in Europe. South and east of the Dardanelles, the Sea of Marmara and the Bosphorus stretches the peninsula known as Asia Minor or Anatolia. Eight thousand two hundred ten kilometers of its border are shores lined with fertile plains; these rise quickly to the high, dry, central plateau where nineteen mountains including the highest, Mt. Ararat, are over 3,500 meters high. The country has three main temperate climates: Mediterranean in the south, Black Sea in the north, and steppe throughout most of Anatolia.

There are four large natural lakes: Van (3,738 km^2), Tuz (1,642 km^2), Beyşehir (650 km^2), and Eğridir (486 km^2). Two large, man-made lakes on the Euphrates River back up behind the Keban and Atatürk Dams. A number of its rivers were well known in antiquity: Euphrates (Fırat), Tigris (Dicle), Halys (Kızılırmak), Araxes (Aras), Sangarius (Sakarya), Sarus (Seyhan), Meander (Büyük Menderes) and Pyramus (Ceyhan).

The capital of Turkey is Ankara located in central Anatolia. The ten main cities in order of their size are Istanbul, Ankara, İzmir, Adana, Bursa, Gaziantep, Konya, Eskişehir, Kayseri and Diyarbakır. The country is divided into provinces *(il* or *vilayet),* each administered by a nationally appointed governor *(vali)* and administration, and a locally elected municipal government *(belediye).* Currently (1997) there are 80 provinces. In 1950 the population numbered about 20 million; by the turn of the century it is estimated that the population will be 67 million.

BIBLICAL SITES IN TURKEY

More than fifty percent of the labor force is engaged in agriculture. The main cash crops include tobacco (Turkey is the world's sixth largest producer), cereals, cotton, olive oil, mohair, wool, silk, figs, raisins, nuts, fruits, opium, gum, and sugar. Antimony, borate, copper, and chrome are mined in sufficient quantities to be exported. In recent years a number of industries have become important in the national economy. These include food and beverages, clothing and cloth manufacture, chemicals, ceramics, and motor vehicles.

GOVERNMENT

The Republic of Turkey (Türkiye Cumhuriyeti) is a democratic, secular, social state. The first president was Mustafa Kemal Atatürk, elected in 1923 following the overthrow of the Ottoman Empire. A new constitution was ratified in November 1982. According to it, the executive power of the government is exercised by the president (elected for one term of seven years) and the Council of Ministers. The legislative power is vested in the Grand National Assembly, a body of 550 deputies elected every five years by vote of all Turkish citizens over the age of 18. Judicial power resides in independent courts responsible to the constitution and to the laws of the land. The Council of State is the last instance for reviewing decisions and judgments given by the administrative courts.

MONETARY UNIT

The monetary unit of Turkey is the lira. There are some metal coins, but most of the money is in paper bills. Some transactions are handled electronically. The value of the lira floats in relation to international currencies.

LANGUAGE

Turkish is one of the Turkic languages used in the Middle East, and is thought to have originated in Central Asia where the first known Turkish tribes were living. It is an agglutinated language; that is, short root words are modified in meaning by the addition of suffix on top of suffix. Thus the root word *gel* means "come"; *gelmedi* is "he did not come." With other additions, the single

Turkish word may need a complicated clause for its translation into English.

Since 1928 Turkish has been written in a phonetic, Latin alphabet of twenty-nine letters. With only few variations the pronunciation is like English. However, each letter represents only one sound. The vowel sounds are the *a* of *father;* the *e* of edit; the *ı*, of the unaccented *e* of *the;* the *i,* the *ee* of feet; the *o* of *so,* the *ö,* of the German word schön; the *u,* the *oo* of pool; and the *ü* the German grün. Consonants that differ are the *c* pronounced as the *j* of *j*ack, the *ç* as ch, the *ğ* which is silent and usually lengthens the previous vowel, the *j* as the *g* of *g*endarme, and the *ş* as sh. Syllables within a word are only lightly accented, if at all. All letters are pronounced. Thus Side (a port on the Mediterranean) has two syllables.

3

RELIGION

While Turkey is a secular state, about ninety-eight percent of the people are Muslims; their faith is that of Islam. "Islam" means "submission;" a Muslim is one who submits himself to God. The great prophet of Islam is Muhammed who lived from about 570 to 632 A.D. Islam dates its beginnings from his pilgrimage from Mecca to Medina in 622 A.D. The holy book of Islam is the Koran which is believed to have been dictated by God to Muhammed. The buildings in which Muslims gather to worship are called mosques (*cami* in Turkish); however a Muslim may worship by performing his prayers any place as long as he and the ground are clean and he faces Mecca. The Muslim calendar is based on twelve lunar months and is therefore ten or eleven days shorter than the solar year. This means that the months and the religious holidays fall a bit earlier each year and thus move through the Gregorian (western) calendar a full cycle in about thirty-three years.

There are five requirements of Islam:

1. Once in one's life one must state with full understanding and acceptance that there is no diety but God and that Muhammed is his prophet.

2. One must pray five times a day at particular intervals. The muezzin's call to prayer from the minaret of the mosque announces these times of prayer.

3. One must observe Ramazan, the month of fasting, during which one neither eats nor drinks anything from the time in the early morning that a white thread can be distinguished from a black one until sunset that evening. This restriction includes smoking.

4

4. One must give alms.

5. Once in one's life one must, if at all possible, make a pilgrimage to Mecca to be there for the Festival of Sacrifice.

The non-Muslim minority people are concentrated in Istanbul. There are Sephardic Jews and Christians of several backgrounds: Greek Orthodox, Armenian Orthodox (the patriarchates of both are located there), Greek Catholic, Syrian Orthodox, a few Protestants, and some others. There are also a few Christian communities around Diyarbakır.

ATATÜRK REFORMS

The first president of Turkey was Mustafa Kemal Atatürk. His professed aim was "Peace at home, peace abroad." Under his leadership the Turkish heart of the defunct Ottoman Empire was consolidated into a geographic, linguistic, and political unity able to exist in the stresses of the modern world. He accomplished this through a number of reforms, most of which were brought about by government decisions.

Many of the reforms can be listed under the general heading of secularization. In addition to the state being proclaimed a secular one in 1928, the caliphate (the office of the spiritual and civil head of Islam) was abolished in 1924, all schools (religious and otherwise) were put under the Ministry of Education, dervish orders were banned, and the Koran was read publicly in Turkish beginning in 1932. The şeriat (Islamic canonical law) was replaced in

1926 by Turkish law based on the Swiss civil law code, the Italian penal code, and the German and Italian commercial codes. Under this new law for instance marriage became a civil contract, and all Turkish citizens came under one code, not under the *millet* (ethnic and religious nationality) system of Ottoman Empire. The international, Gregorian calendar replaced the Islamic calendar and Sunday became the day of rest. In 1928 a modified Latin alphabet was introduced, and the Arabic-based *Osmanlıca* writing was forbidden in any public place.

5

A Turkish Linguistic Society *(Türk Dil Kurumu)* was founded in 1932 to purify and simplify the language in the interest of helping unify the people. Surnames were required in 1934 and old titles indicating professions and classes were dropped. European dress was adopted, the most dramatic instance being the day in 1925 that Atatürk donned a *şapka* — a hat with a brim symbolizing Western infidels — and declared that from then on the *fez* was outlawed. The metric system was adopted in 1934 and by then full franchise was extended to women. The election in 1935 sent seventeen women deputies to the Congress in Ankara. Education through fifth grade was made obligatory; through university public education is still free. Peoples's Houses were set up throughout the country to improve conditions and to teach nationalism, solidarity, secularization, and westernization. The remarkable changes in Turkey since 1923 attest to the effectiveness of these reforms.

HISTORY

Archeological excavations around Antalya and Konya have produced evidence of a Neolithic civilization here dating back to at least 8000 B.C. Remains of pre - Hittite and Hittite peoples have been found in central Anatolia for the time around 2000 B.C., but written history here begins with records from Assyrian traders about 1900 B.C. The Hittite Empire was at its height under Suppiluliumas around 1380 B.C. and then was overthown by the

Phrygians. The Cimmerii ended that power sometime in the ninth or eighth century B.C. and in turn were supplanted by the Lydian kingdom until 546 B.C. when Cyrus the Persian captured its capital, Sardis. Of course all of these kingdoms and empires had ill-defined and transient boundaries, and others, too, including the Urartu and Armenian, were co-existent.

6   Alexander the Great invaded Asia Minor in 334 B.C., and following his death the Seleucid kings took over. By 133 B.C. "Asia" (the plains watered by the Cayster River where the Ionians first settled) was a Roman province. Under pressure from the invading barbarians. Constantine moved his capital from Rome to Byzantium in 330 A.D. and his city, Constantinople, remained the center of the Byzantine Empire until its capture by Sultan Mehmet II in 1453.

In the meantime the Selçuk Turks had invaded Anatolia from the east and in 1071 defeated and captured the Byzantine Emperor Romanus IV Diogenes at the Battle of Manzikert. In 1080 they took Nicaea. Another Turkish tribe was involved in local skirmishes by the 1200s. (It was in this period, also, that the Crusades took place.) Their leader, Süleyman, drowned crossing the Euphrates in 1227. By 1288 his grandson, Osman I, had won his independence from the Selçuk leader, Ala-ud-din Kaikubad II. The Ottoman Empire takes its name from this Osman. Except for the ravages of Tamerlane (1336-1405) who captured Sultan Beyazit I in the battle at Ankara in 1402, the Ottoman Empire grew steadily in area and might, culminating in the reign of Süleyman the Magnificent from 1520 to 1566. At its height the Ottoman Empire extended from the gates of Vienna to the Red Sea and from the Persian Gulf to Algeria. In 1923 the Republic of Turkey was proclaimed as the five hundred years of Ottoman rule were replaced by a constitutional government.

Here in this country is the meeting of the Western and Eastern worlds. The Turkish Republic is but one in a long history of hybrid cultures, an on-going experiment in taking from the East and the West the qualities which will serve its citizens today. Geography, history, and religion are elements of the flux out of which people shape their culture. This flux is continually flowing and fusing as Turks respond to their needs and to the interplay of those with the rest of the world.

CHAPTER II

ANATOLIA IN THE TIME OF THE OLD TESTAMENT

SELECTED REFERENCES:

Descendents of Noah : Genesis 10, 11; I Chronicles 1:1-28
Ararat : Genesis 8:4
Minni : Jeremiah 51:27
Sepharad :Obadiah 20-21
Coa : I Kings 10:28; Ezekiel 23:23

INTRODUCTION

Turkey, particularly Asiatic Turkey known as Anatolia, has inherited within its borders the sites of several crucial events in both Old and New Testament history. Noah's children, according to Genesis, and the animals he saved in the ark began the repopulation of the earth from "a mountain in Ararat;" Abraham's call to greatness came in Harran; and "it was in Antioch that the disciples first got the name of Christians" (Acts 11:26). Ararat is in eastern, Harran in southern, and Antioch in southwestern Turkey.

The peoples who have lived here and those who have passed across the land have been part of the matrix out of which first Judaism and then Christianity developed. Archeologists have found that Hittites, Urartians, Assyrians, and many other nations who were important in the Old Testament were active here as well as farther south. King Tiglath-pileser III of Assyria conquered not only Israel but also Urartu. In 717 B.C. his son, King Sargon II, added Carchemish, which had been a Hittite kingdom, to his estate. Sargon's son, King Sennacherib who fought King Hezekiah, sacked Tarsus in 696 B.C. The people in the Bible who have left records of their activities in Anatolia span the ages from Noah to Paul.

BIBLICAL SITES IN TURKEY

Biblical interpreters have concentrated their attention on events more immediate to Palestine than Turkey. But scholars are increasingly bringing to light details of the complex interrelations among the throngs of people throughout the history of this entire area. Their discoveries show the frequent comings and goings all across the land, the commerce and cultural exchanges, the rich natural resources, and the nations' struggles with their warring neighbors. Names which once were obscure references have now become real people, their homes places to visit and study. Their lives continue to have meaning for us centuries later. We cannot claim a full right to our heritage without acknowledging the contributions of the land and the people of Turkey from time immemorial.

THE LAND

The physical setting of Anatolia has immeasurably influenced the history of the country. It is a land bridge between East and West, between North and South, a part of the triangle linking Europe, Asia, and Africa. For thousands and thousands of years it has been enriched by and has itself enriched the life which has marched across it. It is blessed by its hospitable physical geography: seasonal variations in climate with enough rainfall to favor primitive agriculture, enough animal life to supply good meat and fish, and enough of the hard rocks like quartz, obsidian, and flint for tools. Because of this, much of human development during the Neolithic Revolution from mere hunter to conscious cultivator took place here on the slopes of the Taurus, the Amanus, and the Zagros Mountains where agriculture rather than pasturage was more suitable. Perhaps the drama of this revolution is reflected in the ancient tragedy of Cain the farmer and Abel the herdsman, a tragedy acted out so often that it was transformed from ballad to legend to scripture (Gen.4).

Here also in Anatolia rise two of the rivers which bounded Eden. Lake Hazar just south of Elazığ in the

Taurus Mountains is the source of the Tigris. The Euphrates comes from snows and rains that fall on the mountains in eastern Turkey and join together in the man-made lake at Keban west of Elaziğ (Gen. 2: 10-14). Not far south of this same Elaziğ, in sight of the Tektek Mountains and between the two rivers, is the town of Harran from whence Abraham and his family started on their journey to Canaan (Gen. 12:4)

The eastern and northeastern coastal area of the Mediterranean Sea with its many harbors and fertile plains has been and still is a major commercial highway. Wood, tin, flint, purple dye, and shells were among the first items traded. The purple dye extracted from mollusks is itself a symbol of the wealth of the seacoast: it was used for priests' clothing, tabernacle furnishings, and kingly robes. Canaan, the promised land, meant also the land of this purple dye.

11

THE PEOPLES

While the land has carried the potential for its use, it is the peoples who have lived here who have developed it. Among the many others, the Mediterranean area has harbored Egyptian, Persian, Hittite, Minoan, Greek, and Roman cultures. Each of these has contributed to the fact that this was the center of the most powerful and most complex culture that had developed up to the time of Christ. The spread of Christianity is related directly to the extension of the influence of this culture. Ideas concerning religion and philosophy, commerce, politics, language and writing, astronomy and astrology, navigation, agriculture, law, warfare, and mathematics contributed to the dynamics of this culture as each group borrowed from the others and added its own interpretation.

Variety, pageantry, imagination — good and evil — have colored all the history of the area from earliest times. Other places in the world also claim early records of the human development as inventor, thinker, recorder, and moralist; and only some of the places that are important because of events recorded in the Bible are located within the borders of Turkey. However, this bridge carried and still continues to carry the trade in goods and ideas from East to West and back again. This interplay among people is a part of the fascination which Asia Minor holds in perpetuity.

It is particularly the peoples who are mentioned in the Old Testament whom this chapter and the next touch on. Genesis, one of the earliest recorded and preserved records, gives an account of the interrelationships of the nations of the world as they were perceived by its writers. It is drawn up on the assumption that everyone is a descendent of one or another of the three sons of Noah: Shem, Ham, or Japheth (Gen.10). By grouping nations under these three, the writers sketch out a pattern of relationships. The descendents of Shem are roughly the west Semites; those of Ham roughly the Hamitic groups of Egypt, Ethiopia, and East Africa, plus Babylon, Nineveh, the Assyrians, and the Canaanites. The peoples to the north and west of the writers seem to be the descendents of Japheth. Some of those listed under each group appear to have been related to the ancient inhabitants of Anatolia.

THE NAMES

The names are a blend of place names, tribal names, and the names of persons, presumably the reputed founders of the various nations. However, the purpose of the writers of Genesis was not that of a geography lesson as much as we might wish it to be so for this book. Therefore the details which we might expect in an account today were muted in the writers' concern for establishing the concept of Israel as a chosen people.

Most of us who visit Turkey are not expecting to become linguists. But a few points about the languages of the Near East will help show how names can be traced through the records of differing peoples. Proper names tend to have a longer life than the people who coined them; thus they are useful bits of evidence for archeologists. One of the cues in establishing interrelations is the point that the words in the Semitic languages (Hebrew, Arabic, Aramaic, Akkadian, Phoenician, etc.) have a three-letter root that is modified with varying vowels, prefixes and/or suffixes. Thus "grm" in the Bible is Togarmah; in Assyrian texts it is Tilgarimmu or Tegarama; and today it is quite possibly the Turkish city of Gürün between Sivas and Malatya. Of course the similarity in the words is not the only factor deciding relationships: there a Seleucia north of the Sea of Galilee, another on the mouth of the Orontes River, a third on the mouth of the Calycadnus River, and a fourth on the Tigris River just south of Baghdad. They were all named for one of Alexander the Great's generals who did not have the same trouble keeping them separated that we do today. The similarity carries the possibility of deception also: many names, although they have survived, have been transferred from places they once identified to others elsewhere.

13

DESCENDENTS OF NOAH

"These are the descendents of the sons of Noah, Shem, Ham, and Japheth, the sons born to them after the flood... and from them came the separate nations on earth" (Gen. 10:1-32).

The purpose of the writers of this genealogy, known as the Table of Nations, was to drive home the thesis that Israel was both a chosen and a choosing people. They intended to prove that the entire history of Israel was that of a people with whom God had covenanted and that God worked through history. Israel's favored position, if it had one, was because it remained faithful to God. From Adam through Seth, Noah, Shem, and later on through Isaac, Jacob, Judah, Boaz, Jesse, and David, God had shaped His people. He had given them a law higher than human law, a religious mission and responsibility, and an immortal destiny.

The writers not only credited Noah with being one of the progenitors of the Hebrews (through Eber), but also listed a number of unlikely relatives for them. World history, and particularly the historical influence of those peoples that Israel came in contact with, was seen as a whole. The germ of the thought of universality developed

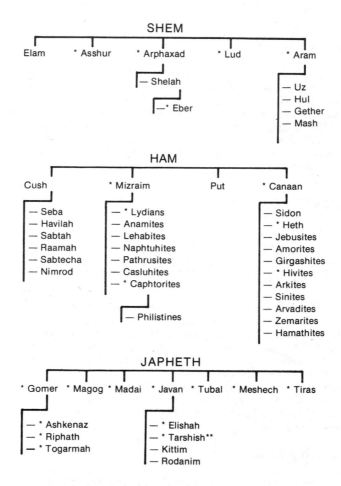

*These may have connections in Turkey.
** Possibly it is Tarshish of the Kittim.

in the Old Testament writers until it grew into the statement in Isaiah, "... now the Lord calls me again: it is too slight a task for you, as my servant, to restore the tribes of Jacob, to bring back the descendents of Israel: I will make you a light to the nations, to be my salvation to earth's farthest bounds" (Is. 49:5-6).

Of the names of the descendents of Noah, some seem to have a relationship with people who have lived in Anatolia. Some of the places the people such as the Hittites and the Mushki lived and some of their buildings have been identified by archeologists working in the last hundred years. This work continues every year as more and more cuneiform-inscribed seals and black-glazed potsherds are uncovered and fitted into the pattern of the early history and movements of people of the Near East. The Bible is one of the archeologists' major references as they search to understand what they find and where to look for more pieces of the puzzle. One of their interesting discoveries is that many of our customs and beliefs that are recorded in the Bible are also discernible through the fragments of the lives that these people left behind them. Thus Anatolia has been an important field for confirming, correcting, and enriching our knowledge.

By families, the people referred to in the Bible and speculatively identified as living in or passing through Anatolia are the following. Those of Noah's relations are given first, then those who are mentioned in other biblical passages are identified. The distinctions among the groups often get lost, perhaps partly because the groups themselves did not have rigid boundaries or identities, partly because they intermarried, partly because our own knowledge of them is incomplete and in some cases wrong. Many of them did not stay put, either.

SHEM'S FAMILY—THE SEMITES

Noah's first son was Shem. Four of his sons, Asshur, Arphaxad, Lud, and Aram, and their offspring may have been important in the history of Anatolia.

.15

ASSHUR

Asshur was the ancestor from whom the Assyrians were reputed to have gotten their name. They lived in what is now Iraq between the Tigris and Euphrates Rivers. The northern area of their influence extended into southern Turkey as they came in contact with Hittites, Hurrians, Mitanni, and later the Greeks when Alexander the Great penetrated Mesopotamia. Two stone-carved Assyrian lions making a double column base from the time of Tiglath-pileser III (eighth century B.C.) were found at a temple in Tell Tainat on the Orontes River. They are now in the Archeological Museum in Antakya. Assyrian traders were important in the commercial life of the Hittite city of Kanesh (Kültepe) north of today's Kayseri. The Assyrian governor of Coa — the fertile Adana plain — fought the Mushki King Midas in 709 B.C., captured two of his fortresses, and forced him to pay tribute. In the seventh century Assyrians from Nineveh may have been living in what is now known as Aphrodisias. A connection with Nineveh in the cult of Zeus Nineudius is suggested by some inscriptions there.

LUD

Lud as one of Shem's sons presents a problem, in part because of the listing of the Lydians under Ham's son Mizraim. But the Lydians or the Ludians who lived largely around Izmir and Sardis were not any more Semites than they were Hamites. (The confusion suggests that the authors of the Table of Nations in Genesis and I Chronicles knew the areas and peoples surrounding Palestine more intimately than they did outlying groups, and therefore they were less accurate the farther afield they wandered. It also suggests that we may not know everything about them either. When the Lydians under King Gyges sent an envoy to the Assyrian King Ashurbanipal about 660 B.C. they found they did not have a language in common. They probably also did not know that some people had thought they were cousins. A hundred years later Lydia became part of the Persian Empire when it was conquered by Cyrus in 546 B.C.

OLD TESTAMENT ANATOLIA

ARPHAXAD

Nahor, the seventh generation removed from Shem through Arphaxad (Gen. 11:22-25), is supposed to have lived in the region around Harran. This Nahor is the father of Terah and the grandfather of Abraham. One theory suggests that Harran rather than the area around Ur of the Chaldees may have been the place where the Hebrew family got started.*

ARAM
17

The youngest of Shem's sons, Aram, and his family of Arameans were scattered throughout Mesopotamia, Syria, and into southern Anatolia. Aram-naharaim, the Aram of the Two Rivers, may be Harran; Padan-Aram, the road or the plain of Aram, perhaps is the area from Harran south.

The area around Diyarbakır and on the east spurs of Karaca Dağ may be the original land of Arame. Bit Zamani is an early Aramaic site on the south bank of the Tigris River near Diyarbakır. Farther west near Gaziantep lay the Aramean state of Sam'al whose capital Zincirli (near Fevzipaşa) commanded the pass across the mountains into Cilicia. King Hezekiah was reminded of the fate of this country and others who opposed the Assyrians (II Kings 18:33-35) when King Sennacherib demanded the surrender of Jerusalem. The sculpture found at Zincirli and presently in the Archeological Museum in Istanbul shows the mastery of the eighth century B.C. artists. Two mythological winged animals with human heads stood once as a column base; now they represent the combined inspiration of Neo-Hittites, Arameans, and Assyrians.

Arameans borrowed the simple Phoenician alphabet of shapes representing consonant sounds, transformed it into an even more efficient tool, and to our great debt passed it on to all those with whom they came in contact. The use of Aramaic for diplomatic exchanges is referred to in II Kings 18:26. Aramaic script is the source of the Greek and Latin alphabets among many others.

* See the recent work on the discoveries at Ebla: **The Archives of Ebla** by Giovanni Pettinato.

HAM'S FAMILY — THE HAMITES

Ham is the second of Noah's three sons. His own sons are given as Cush, Mizraim, Put, and Canaan. Cush has been located as the people living south of the Red Sea; Mizraim was those in Egypt; Canan included people living to the northwest of Palestine but stretching into Africa; and Put perhaps was the people living in Libya.

18

The listing has several problems with the groups that may have associations in Anatolia. For instance, if the Mizraim people were those living in Egypt, then do the Lydians of Asia Minor and the Philistines belong in this ﹂grouping? Or were these both a part of the Sea People who migrated from the north into Palestine, continued on south in about 1200 B.C., and left a dark age of several hundred years in their wake?

Something of the same problems applies to those related to Canaan. "Canaanite" appears originally to have meant the Mediterranean coast people who manufactured or traded in the purple dye which was made from snails. Sidon and Phoenicia also may have meant purple. The Arvadites and the Zemarites seem to have lived in the coastal area around Tripoli and to have been engaged in the trade in this same dye. It was a major industry. But other Canaanites, Heth (the Hittites) and the Hivites (who may be the Horites or Hurrians) seem to have moved into the country farther northeast in Central Anatolia. As with many other family relationships, this one is confusing.

MIZRAIM

The Lydians

The Lydians, who seem to be children of Ham through Mizraim in this listing (see Shem's family above), lived in the country of western Anatolia. Their capital was Sardis. The Hittite word, Assuwa, which later became the name Asia, may have referred to Lydia. There are a few Hittite monuments in the area, among them the bas-relief of a warrior near Karabel in the mountains about thirty kilometers east of Izmir.

OLD TESTAMENT ANATOLIA

The Caphtorites

Caphtor, the place from where the Philistines came according to Genesis and Jeremiah (47:4), is located on the Island of Crete by some Egyptologists. Others say it was the Egyptian city of Coptus. Or perhaps it may have been a coastal area of Asia Minor. In the Canaanite language "Caphtorian" means "Aegean."

CANAAN

Heth

Of Canaan's family, Heth is supposed to be the progenitor of the Hittites. They lived in Central Anatolia and were an important group from about the turn of the second millennium B.C. until 717 B.C. when the Assyrian King Sargon II defeated the last remnants of their power at Carchemish.

At the height of the Hittite kingdom during the time of King Suppuliumas the capital was at Hattusas, east of present-day Ankara and known now as Boğazkale. His fame was recognized by one of the queen-widows of Egypt (? Nefertiti) who wrote to him asking for one of his sons to become her husband. Suppiluliumas died in 1335 B.C. of the plague which had been carried to Anatolia by Egyptian prisoners of war. Kanesh near Kayseri, Beycesultan between Denizli and Afyonkarahisar, Carchemish south of Gaziantep, Tyana south of Niğde, and Eski Malatya were also important centers.

The Hittites are mentioned many times in the Old Testament, some in reference to people living in Palestine and some to those with whom the Hebrews had dealings outside. Abraham bought a place to bury Sarah from the Hittite Ephron (Gen.23). To the distress of Isaac and Rebecca (Gen. 26:34-35), Esau married two Hittite girls; they sent Jacob back to Harran (Gen. 27:46; 28:1-2) to keep him from doing the same thing. Ahimelech the Hittite was one of David's advisors when David stole Saul's spear and water jar while Saul slept (I Sam.26:6). Uriah and his wife Bathsheba were Hittites (II Sam. 11-12). King

Solomon the lover married at least one Hittite out of his seven hundred wives (I Kings 11:1). King Solomon the canny ruler was in the import-export business of horses and chariots with the Hittite and Aramean kings (I Kings 10:26-29). Later he employed them, the Amorites, the Terizzites, the Hivites, and the Jebusites as forced labor in public works (II Chron. 8:7-9). Ezekiel (16:1-4) scolds Jerusalem (the home of the Jebusites) saying, "Canaan is the land of your ancestry and there you were born; an Amorite was your father and a Hittite your mother." Presumably Ezekiel's meaning was figurative, but the passage underlines the intermixture among the various peoples which persists to this day.

20

The Hittite people spoke an Indo-European language. The inflections of their nouns closely parallel Latin and Greek, and some of their words are clearly related. For instance, "water" was "watar", "what" (in Latin, "quid") was "quit." The Hittites taught the people of Crete the use of clay tablets for keeping records. They also mined iron, a metal which at one time was more precious than gold.

The Hivites (Hurrians)

The word "Hivite" has caused a puzzle for scholars because the letters "r" and "v" in Hebrew are quite similar and can be confused. Thus perhaps the people referred to as Hivites (Ex. 3:17) are those we speak of today as Hurrians. They should not be identified with the Horites from Seir, but they do seem to be related to the Jebusites of Jerusalem.

Hurrians probably came originally from far eastern Turkey, Armenian Russia, and northwestern Iran. They spread into Anatolia, south into Palestine, and farther on into Egypt. A number of tablets in the Hurrian language discovered at Boğazkale indicate the Hurrian influence there in the middle of the second millennium B.C.* These and other Hurrian records such as those from Nuzi in Iraq are contributing greatly to understanding the backgrounds of customs, interrelations, and language of the biblical people.

* Gelb, Ignace J., **Hurrians and Subarians,** p. 68

The Hurrian people established the Mitanni Empire which included Assyria and was at its height from the middle of the third millennium B.C. to the end of the second. Today's Urfa was one of the political centers of this kingdom. Its western border was the Euphrates River where it met the Egyptian Empire of Thutmose III in the fifteenth century B.C. Hurrians were Indo-Aryans who fought from horse-drawn chariots, an innovation which gave them a military advantage. Their art, language, and literature have left marks on the cultures of the area which scholars are still studying.

JAPHETH'S FAMILY — THE JAPHETHITES

Japheth is named last in the list of Noah's sons. Perhaps he was thought of as the youngest. His own sons are supposedly the ancestors of many tribes living to the north and west of the Hebrews in areas close to Mt. Ararat. Most of them now would be called Indo-Europeans.

GOMER

Gomer is Japheth's oldest son. The name in Greek is associated with the Cimmarians, a nomadic group who lived in southern Russia and spread south from there and west into Europe. They invaded Asia Minor from the eighth to the sixth centuries B.C. In the eighth and seventh centuries they attacked Urartu (causing King Rusa I to commit suicide), Tubal, and the Phrygians (Meshech — burning Gordium and causing its King Midas to commit suicide also). They were finally put down by Alyattes of Lydia, the father of Croesus, sometime near the beginning of the sixth century B.C. They are mentioned by Heroditus, by Homer, and in Assyrian inscriptions. Their wars seem to have been more hit and run raids than defenses of strong fortifications because no towns or castles belonging to them have been found yet. There may be a connection between the Cimmarians who moved to western Europe, the Celts, and the Galatians who invaded central Turkey in the third century B.C.

Gomer's three sons were Ashkenaz, Riphath, and Togarmah.

Ashkenaz

Ashkenaz was a kingdom located in the general area of southern Russia and northeastern Turkey. The people seem to have also been a nomadic group known as the Scythians who pushed the Cimmarians to invade Asia Minor. The Scythians, the Minni and the Assyrians fought in varying combinations. At one time the Scythians were allies of the Assyrians; at another they seem to have helped bring them and the Urartu kingdom down. Later they continued their raids down the Mediterranean coast as far as Egypt. They were defeated and killed off by the Medes, those people related to Japheth's third son, Madai.

Riphath

Riphath is probably an Anatolian tribe that may have been located around the southwest corner of the Black Sea and the Asian side of the Bosphorus. Riphath is thought by some to be the father of the Celts; some also associate the name with Paphlagonia, the Roman province on the Black Sea.

Togarmah

Togarmah probably was a group living around present-day Gürün north of Malatya. They may have been known in Cappadocia under the name of Gamir. In Ezekiel's dirge about Tyre (Ezek. 27:14), he says, "Men from Togarmah offered horses, mares, and mules as your staple wares." Togarmah was destroyed by the Assyrians in 695 B.C.

MAGOG

Japheth's second son was Magog. Magog has been identified with the Scythians (along with Ashkenaz) who lived north and northeast of the Black Sea and who were much feared in the sixth century B.C. Magog is called the land from which Gog came, "the prince of Rosh, Meshech, and Tubal" (Ezek. 38:2). There has been much debate about whether Magog was a real place and Gog a real king or not, or whether they were representations of the powers of evil. Gog was expected to join with Gomer, Togarmah, Tarshish, and others against Israel, but be utterly destroyed and "buried in the Valley of Gog's Horde" (Ezek. 39:15).

23

MADAI

Japheth's third son, Madai, is identified with the Medes who lived in present-day northwest Iran. The Cimmarians and the Scythians came in contact with them frequently, and they skirmished with the Assyrians also. During the time of Jeremiah, the Median Empire extended well into central Anatolia. In 585 B.C. Cyaxares the Mede who had invaded Urartu and Cappadocia and Alyattes the Lydian had fought to a stalemate. Nebuchadrezzar the Assyrian negotiated the truce between them and fixed their common border on the Halys River (Kızılırmak). Nebuchadrezzar perhaps had a special interest in the arrangements because his wife was a Median princess. Cyrus the Mede defeated Croesus at Sardis in 546 B.C. Darius the Mede Built the first bridge (of boats) across the Bosphorus in 512 B.C.

JAVAN

Javan, Japheth's fourth son, as a place is presumably Ionia, the northwestern coast of Anatolia. Thrace, Macedonia and the Aegean Islands. In the Bible the application of the term is to the whole Greek-speaking world. Isaiah names Javan, Tubal, Meshech, Lud, Tarshish, Put and Rosh as the "distant coasts and islands" which in the future will see and announce God's glory among the nations (Isa. 66:19). Joel talks about the Greeks who are in the slave business and have carried the people of Israel away from their home (Joel 3:6); Ezekiel mentions them involved in slave trade also (Ezek. 27:13). Javan's family included Elishah, Tarshish, Kittim, and Rodanim.

Like Ham's family of the Canaanites, Javan's Elishah family seems to have been connected with the export trade in purple dye. They also carried the name Alashiya which appears in cuneiform records in Ugarit between the eighteenth and thirteenth centuries B.C. (Ugarit was an important city state on the Mediterranean coast just north of Latakia. During its heyday it showed Amorite, Hittite, Hurrian, Egyptian, and Mycenean influences until it was destroyed by the Sea People in the twelfth century B.C.)

Perhaps the people of Elishah lived around Tyre, perhaps in Cyprus, but probably not in Turkey. They exported copper to Babylon as early as the eighteenth century B.C.

Tarshish

Tarshish has not been identified with any certainty. In Isaiah 2:16 it appears as a distant, idealized place. Speculation on its location includes identifying it with one of the Levantine ports such as Tarsus in southern Turkey or with Tartessus in Spain. Its residents exported silver, iron, tin, and lead (Ezek. 27:12). Jonah was once intending to sail from Joppa to Tarshish (Jonah 1:3), but God had other plans for him.

Kittim is the Hebrew word for Cyprus. Rodanim is probably Rhodes.

TUBAL

In Assyrian records Tubal or Tabal seems to be located in the Cappadocian plain. It or its capital may have been at Kayseri. Tubal was perhaps the founder of Tarsus. During the ninth and eighth centuries B.C. it was politically an important region. Tabal and Meshech (Mushki) traded in bronze and copper with Assyria. Towards the end of the eighth century the Tabal King Ambaris was involved with Mushki and Urartu groups against the Assyrian King Sargon II who was the father of Sennacherib.

MESHECH

Meshech appears to be securely identified as the Mushki of Assyrian records. The earliest references to them are from time of the Assyrian King Tiglath-pileser I who beat five of their kings about 1100 B.C. The land of the Mushki was in central Anatolia; their capital at Gordium was destroyed by the Cimmarians in 695 B.C. The most numerous references to the Mushki date from the time of the Assyrian King Sargon II who was a major enemy of their King Mita (known in Greek as King Midas). Through the Assyrian records we know that King Mita was an ally of King Ambaris of Tubal and King Rusa of Urartu (Ararat). This king's name, "Mita," is carved into the rocks in the Hittite temple at Yazılı Kaya.

TIRAS

Tiras, the last of Japheth's sons, is less positively identified. Perhaps the reference is the same as the "Sea People" in the Egyptian records at the time of Ramses III.

Another theory is that they are the elusive Etruscans who came to Italy from Asia Minor about the ninth century B.C. Heroditus says they migrated from Lydia because of a famine. Much of the early Etruscan art work shows a similarity to Assyrian designs, so the Anatolian background is a plausible one.

Josephus adds to the puzzle concerning Japheth's son saying, "Thiras also called those whom he ruled over Thirasian; but the Greeks changed the name into Thracians."* Thrace covered what is parts of Greece and Bulgaria and all of European Turkey.

* Josephus, **Antiquities of the Jews,** Bk. I, ch. 6

Thus, although the concrete data in hand at present are insufficient and sometimes self-contradictory, it appears that many of the members of Noah's family according to the lists in Genesis and Chronicles have left their marks in early Turkish history: Shem's sons Asshur (the Assyrians), Arphaxad (Nahor's and Abraham's family in Harran), Lud (? the Lydians), and Aram (the Arameans); Ham's sons Mizraim (?· the Lydians and the Caphtorites) and Canaan (Heth and the Hivites); and Japheth's sons Gomer (the Cimmarians), Magog (the Scythians), Madai (the Medes), Javan (the Ionians), Tubal (in Cappadocia), Meshech (the Mushki), and Tiras (? the Thracians or Etruscans).

REFERENCES OUTSIDE THE TABLE OF NATIONS

A few references in the Old Testament to countries and people not included in Noah's family have connections with Anatolia: the Urartu, the Minni, the Sepharad, and the people of Coa.

ARARAT

Ararat (or in Assyrian, Urartu) was located around Mt. Ararat (Gen. 8:4) and Lake Van; the area extended through present-day eastern Turkey, southwestern Russia, and northern Iran. Its inhabitants called themselves Chaldini, although Chaldea usually refers to a region south of Babylon. It was an important country in the ninth century B.C. with a population of at least 50,000 people when King Sarduri I established his capital in Van. A hundred years later its King Sarduri III was defeated by the Assyrian King Tiglath-pileser III. King Sarduri retreated to his capital, Tushpa (Van), in 735 B.C. A relative of King Sarduri, King Rusa I, established his capital in Toprakkale just southeast of Van. He and King Merodach-baladan of Babylon (Isa. 39:1) were allies against Sargon II. Rusa died in 714 as a result of the

Cimmarian invasion of Urartu which was led by Sargon. The murderers of Sargon's son, Sennacherib, escaped to Urartu (II Kgs. 19:37) according to the biblical account.

The invasions and skirmishes continued among the Cimmarians, the Mushki, the Tubals, the Scythians, and the Medes (Jer. 51:27-28), all of whom had perhaps been pushed west by Hsiung-Nu tribesmen, a Turkic group who by the third century B.C. were the main power north of the Great Wall of China. The Armenians, an Indo-European group who may have lived for a while in Phrygia, became the main group of people around Van about the beginning of the fifth century B.C. The area south of Trabzon appears to have been the last home of the Chaldeans.

27

Urartian, Minoan, and Etruscan arts show enough similarities that it seems probable that they influenced each other. Among the Etruscan contributions to Italian life were the practices of soothsaying and astrology, accomplishments they may have learned in the Near East. Urartian art was at its height as contacts between it and western Anatolia and Greece were developing. Its metal industry was similar to that of Tubal and Gordium with gold, silver, and copper being the main products. Bronze cauldrons with bulls heads like handles on the rims have been found in graves in both Gordium and Altıntepe, an Urartian site near Erzincan.

MINNI

The Minni were a people located in the same area as the Urartu and the Ashkenaz around Mt. Ararat and Lake Van. They appear as the Manneans in Assyrian inscriptions in the middle of the ninth century B.C. God calls on them to wreak vengeance on Babylon in Jeremiah 51:27.

SEPHARAD

Obadiah 20-21 mentions the Sepharad, the exiles of Jerusalem who will be part of the conquering host of the Lord on the Day of Judgment. Probably this is a reference to a Jewish colony living in Sardis. Sardis was an important trading center on the western end of the Royal Road from Susa near the Persian Gulf. Perhaps these exiles were prisoners of war who had been sold as slaves to the Lydians.

COA

28

Solomon imported horses from Coa (I Kgs. 10:28), or Cilicia, the fertile plain in southern Turkey around the city of Adana, but extending as far west as Alanya and as far east as the Amanus Mountains. Lumber from the mountainous area of Coa was famous for its use in ship building.

During the Hittite period in central Anatolia it was an independent country known as Kizzuwatna. In the fourteenth century B.C. under King Suppiluliumas it became one of the Hittite dependencies. Mushki people invaded it in the end of the eighth century, but the Assyrian King Sargon II defeated them and took over the area about 712 B.C. It came under Persian influence for a while, to be followed by Hellenistic and Roman periods.

In Assyrian records Coa is known as Kue.

Almost all of the peoples living in Anatolia are mentioned in one or many connections in the Old Testament. Trade, migration, war, and marriage arrangements brought them together, influenced how they lived and what they thought, and helped them leave their marks on even our history and thought today. How rich our inheritance has been!

CHAPTER III
OLD TESTAMENT LOCATIONS

SELECTED REFERENCES:
Assyrians: II Kings 16:7-9; 18
Harran: Genesis 11:31-34; 12:4-5; 24:10 (?); 27:43; 28:10; 29:4;
  II Kings 19:12; Ezekiel 27:23; Isaiah 37:12
Hivites, Hurrians: Genesis 14:6; 36:20-21; Deuteronomy 2:12
Carchemish: II Chronicles 35:20; Jeremiah 46:2; Isaiah 10:9
Tubal, Meshech: Isaiah 66:19; Psalms 120:5; Ezekiel 38:1-6
Hittites: Genesis 27:46; Exodus 3:17; 23:23-24; Joshua 1:4;
  II Samuel 11:2-3
Togarmah: Ezekiel 38:2
Mt. Ararat, Urartu: Genesis 8:4; Jeremiah 51:27
Sepharad: Obadiah 20, 21
Tigris and Euphrates Rivers: Genesis 2:14; Revelation 9:14;16:12

While the land and its people have certainly changed many times since Noah and Jeremiah, they do retain qualities that remind the modern Westerner that the values in life are not all circumscribed by the demands of efficiency, technology, progress, and speed. As one looks either at the bas-reliefs of Carchemish or at the religious symbols from Alaca Höyük, one is compelled to respect the greatness of mind and the artistry of those people who are among the antagonists in biblical accounts.

Not many specific places mentioned in the Old Testament are points on the map of Turkey which one can visit today. Even those which have been identified may arouse doubts and disappointments of one kind or another for the tourist. If one journeys to Harran expecting to find there the physical remains of Abraham's camp site one is likely to be disillusioned. Although pottery and ruined walls remind us of the work and lives of Abraham and his family, their value is not intrinsic, but rather is in what we can learn from them to apply to ourselves. In that sense this book is only a guide pointing from the past. The richness and the excitement of the land are still here, but perhaps one can find these more in the living people than in the shards that litter the ground.

Each of the members of Noah's family are represented in some way in Anatolia. They have left aqueducts, fortresses, burial mounds, commercial records, bas-reliefs, and even household furnishings. Some of these records, such as pieces of the walls around the city of Carchemish, are still in place; others are best seen in the museums, particularly the Museum of Anatolian Civilizations (Anadolu Medeniyetleri Müzesi) in Ankara. Many of the places in Turkey bear records of more than one member of the family: Hittites, Assyrians, Phrygians (Mushki), Cimmarians, and Lydians contributed to the complicated history of Gordium. Members of other families also known by Old Testament writers, such as the Urartians, can be studied here. Some are known by more than one name. Every year archeologists find more clues to their lives and their effects on their neighbors. Those places that have some concrete evidence which one can see in Anatolia are described briefly here.

CUDİ DAĞI, KARABUR, ZİNCİRLİ

Assyrian reliefs in the rocks have been found at Cudi Dağı in southeastern Turkey near Cizre, and at Karabur in the Province of Hatay, among other places. According to Islamic tradition, Cudi Dağı rather than Mt. Ararat was the resting place of Noah's ark. It is not as high as Ararat, but it is closer to the Tigris River and to a possible flood plain.

Such Assyrian records neither prove nor disprove the location of Noah's mountain, but they do associate the area with names in the Old Testament. The Assyrians, the Babylonians, the Chaldeans, and later the Persians were important throughout Mesopotamia; their economic, military, and religious influence extended from the Persian Gulf deep into Anatolia. While they appear in the Old Testament largely in connection with events that impacted Palestine, records of them are also found in Zincirli, Şanlıurfa, and Kanesh. Among the Assyrian kings whose names echo in history are Tiglath-Pileser III (745-727 BC) whose power was recognized by the kings of Israel (I Chron. 5:26); Sargon II (722-705 BC) whose death in southeastern Turkey may be the subject of Isa. 14:4-21; and Sennacherib (705-681 BC), his son, who fought King Hezekiah of Judah in 701. Later Sennacherib was murdered by two of his own sons who then fled to the region around Lake Van (II Kings 19:37). The Babylonian King Nebuchanezzar II (605-562 BC) defeated the Egyptian Pharaoh Neco at Carchemish in 605. As the Babylonian Empire diminished, the Persian took its place. Cyrus II (539-530 BC) conquered the Lydian kingdom in 537; his name appears in Daniel, as do the Chaldean magicians and astrologers.

At Karabur there are the symbols of the moon god Sin (a crescent), the sun god Shamash (a winged sun disk), and the war god Asshur (a horned helmet).

Many clay tablets of Assyrian trading accounts (the earliest written records in Anatolia) found at Kanesh (Kültepe) are on display in the Museum of Anatolian Civilizations in Ankara. A stele of King Esarhaddon, the son of Sennacherib, was found in the excavations at

OLD TESTAMENT LOCATIONS

Zincirli near Fevzipaşa. It and other Assyrian items are scattered in museums in Ankara, Istanbul, and around the world.

HARRAN — ALTINBAŞAK

The present town of Altınbaşak is to the side of the ruins of the great stronghold of Harran. Harran is surrounded by a city wall in poor repair although the gates are obvious. A hill in the center would appear to be the site of the earliest settlement; this has not been excavated. Part of the way up the hill on the northwest side is a pair of doorposts with a marker indicating that the place is known as "Aran's House." Tradition says this is the house from which Abraham took Sarah.

Most of the present castle to the southeast is of later date than the walls which it interrupts. There is evidence of Hittite influence in its foundations, and the possibility that it marks the site of one of the temples to the moon-god, Sin. But most of what one sees there is eleventh and early twelfth century work, the last being during the period of the Crusader Countship of Edessa, 1098 - 1146.

The other striking ruin in Harran is that of the Great Mosque on the north slope of the hill which probably dates from the Omayyad period in the seventh or eighth century A.D. It, too, may be on the site of a much earlier temple. In the mosque courtyard is a very tall square minaret. Some of the broken columns are of a pink marble from the Tektek Dağları; black basalt from north of Urfa was used for occasional stones. On another stone is carved a caduceus.

Altınbaşak is interesting because of the mud brick houses shaped like cones or bee hives some four or five meters high. One reason suggested for this construction is the burning summer sun, the effects of which are somewhat softened by high ceilings.

Harran is known from inscriptions to have been in existence around 2000 B.C. It was an important city in the fourteenth century B.C., the period of the Old Testament patriarchs. Because it lay on the road between Nineveh and the fords of the Euphrates River at Carchemish, it was of great strategic importance.

Harran was also a religious city, one of the centers of the worship of the moon-god Sin. Sin was one of the gods of the Babylonian-Assyrian pantheon, and Harran was the site of perhaps his greatest temples. Their roofs were made from the cedars of Lebanon; they were decorated with lapis lazuli and silver. Sin was usually represented wearing a flowing beard with a crescent above a horned tiara. In later representations only the crescent appears. His worship continued well into the sixth century A.D. in Harran.

Two events of world importance happened in Harran (called Carrhae) in Roman times; first, the army of Rome led by Crassus was almost annihilated in 53 B.C. by the Parthians from the south of the Caspian Sea. Most of an army of 44,000 men were either killed or captured. Of those captured, 10,000 were settled in central Asia as prisoners of war. Crassus himself was not so fortunate. He had been one of the first triumvirate with Pompey and Caesar, and had accepted the province of Syria in the division of the empire. His surname Dives (rich) befit his hopes; he expected that Syria would add considerably to his personal wealth. In 54 B.C. he had helped himself to the treasures in the temple in Jerusalem. But he was among those captured by the Parthians and beheaded by them, according to Plutarch's account of his life.*

The second event involved the Roman Emperor Marcus Aurelius Caracalla who was murdered just outside Harran on April 6 or 8, 217 A.D. as he was returning to the city from worshipping Sin.

The biblical interest in Harran is as one of the probable residences of Abraham and his family. With his father, Terah, he moved here from Ur (Gen. 11:31); and Terah died here. Part of Abraham's family remained after he left for Canaan; he sent back there to find a wife for Isaac. Then later Harran was the place of refuge for Jacob when

32

---

* Plutarch: **Crassus,** par. 31.

Haran

Ararat

34

Boğazkale

Alacahöyük

Edessa

Euphrat

Tigris

Geserkalender

Göreme

Perge

Patara

39

Museum von Konya

Antiochia in Pisidien

Milet

Esau was threatening to kill him. Jacob's Well (Bi'r Yakub) a bit more than a kilometer west of the walls has been the source of drinking water for Harran and the neighboring villages as it traditionally was when Rebecca drew water for Abraham's servant (Gen. 24) and when Jacob helped Rachel (Gen. 29:10) roll the stone off and water Laban's sheep.

EDESSA — URFA

The city of Urfa dates back to the second millennium B.C. when it may have been the capital of a Hurrian state. It has been known variously as Orrhoe, Orhai, and Osrhoene. The word "Hurri" has survived in these various forms of the name of the city. Abraham's name in Chaldean was "Orham"; it may point to a similar relationship.

A spring at the foot of the citadel feeds pools of fish — sacred carp, according to Muslim tradition. This tradition also states that Abraham stopped here. No remains of any great antiquity are visible in the city although there is a thirteenth century square minaret and a seventeenth century Islamic religious school, the Abd-er Rahman Medresesi.

One of the early Christian communities developed here. Their language was not Greek but rather Syriac. According to the early church historian Eusebius, the first church in Edessa began when Jesus answered a plea for help from the king, Abgar. Thus the community claims to be pre-crucifixion in its origin. In the second century A.D. a member of that community, Tatian, produced a Syriac "harmony" of the Gospels which was used in the church there. For fifty years Crusaders held the area in the twelfth century and built a citadel. Within the citadel are two columns on one of which there is a Syriac inscription. These were part of the winter palace of King Abgar.

CARCHEMISH — KARKEMİŞ, BARAK

Carchemish lies a few kilometers south of Birecik on the Euphrates River. Near the village of Barak on the west bank of the river can be found the few ruins of what was once the capital of one of the most powerful of the Hittite kingdoms. The site is on the border between Turkey and Syria and therefore guarded by the army. Because of this one must take a soldier with one as guide and guard when visiting it. While Hattusas, the capital of the Hittite Empire, was still functioning (before 1200 B.C.), Carchemish was dependent upon the northern kings. After the fall of Hattusas, Carchemish was a separate kingdom until it was annexed to Assyria in 717 B.C. by Sargon II. The beauty of Carchemish is in its location on the broad Euphrates and in its art work, some of which is now in the Museum of Anatolian Civilizations in Ankara. Among the items there are reliefs from a wall celebrating a victorious battle against the Assyrians. A driver holds the reins of a horse while an archer shares the platform of the chariot with him and stands poised ready to shoot. Underneath the horse lies a dying enemy. Reliefs illustrating the Gilgamesh Epic (a Babylonian story about a great flood) were also found in Carchemish.

Carchemish was the scene of the battle between the armies of Pharaoh Necho of Egypt and Nebuchadrezzar. Egypt with her mercenaries from Cush (Sudan), Put (Libya), and Lud (western Turkey) was unable to stand against Babylon. While Pharaoh Necho was passing through Judah on his way to the battle with Nebuchadrezzar at Carchemish, Josiah the king of Judah tried to stop him. Necho told Josiah that he had no quarrel with him, but Josiah was shot by Egyptian archers and died from the wound (II Chr. 35:20-25). Necho went on to be defeated by Nebuchadrezzar at Carchemish in 605 B.C.

TUBAL — KAYSERİ

Tubal may be present-day Kayseri. The oldest settlement in Kayseri was probably on a rise slightly southwest of the city where the land slopes up the skirts of Mt. Erciyes. One local tradition supports the idea that a grandson of Noah established a colony there. An early name for the city was Mazaca by which it continued to be known into Byzantine times. (Was this a reference to Meshech?)* It was given the additional name of Caesarea

* Josephus, **Antiquities of the Jews,** Bk. I, ch. 6.

OLD TESTAMENT LOCATIONS

perhaps by the Emperor Tiberius when Cappadocia became a Roman province in 17 A.D., or perhaps a bit later by Claudius when he reorganized the province in 41 A.D. Tubal-Kayseri has almost always been an important city on the commercial route between the Mediterranean and the Black Sea. Unfortunately very little excavation has been done in the immediate environs of Kayseri.

BOĞAZKALE, YAZILI KAYA, ALACA HÖYÜK

Boğazkale, Yazılı Kaya, and Alaca Höyük are archeological sites east of Ankara and north of Yozgat. Boğazkale, the double-walled city above the present village of Boğazköy, was known as Hattusas and was the capital of the Hittite Old Kingdom around 1700 B.C. The Hittites were perhaps the earliest Indo-European peoples to invade central Asia Minor along with the Luwites about 2000 B.C. The area was already settled by proto-Hatti people who spoke an agglutinated language like Sumerian and who produced gold ornaments of remarkable artistry. Fragments of the Gilgamesh Epic written in the Hurrian language were found during excavations at Boğazkale.

Yazılı Kaya, with its bas-reliefs on the living rock, was one of the religious centers of the Hittites, and near it was the burial ground of the people. It is about ten kilometers from Boğazköy.

Alaca Höyük, about forty kilometers by road from Boğazkale, was a royal residence in pre-Hittite times (2400-2200 B.C.). Many silver, bronze, and gold objects have been found there; some were household items, some such as sun discs and figures of stags were objects of worship. These can be seen in the Museum of Anatolian Civilizations in Ankara.

KANESH — KÜLTEPE

Closely related to the events that took place in Kayseri are those that happened in Kanesh (Kültepe) which is twenty kilometers northeast of Kayseri. Kanesh was a major Hittite city where thousands of clay tablets — business letters neatly written on clay, then baked, and then enclosed in neatly inscribed clay envelopes and baked again — have been found with dates beginning about 1850 B.C. So far these are the earliest written documents discovered in Anatolia. They are commercial records of Assyrian traders who lived outside the city walls and dealt in metalwork.

Many clay seals, similar to the tablets, have been found at Kanesh and elsewhere. These are cylindrical beads with a hole through the center so that they could be strung on a cord and worn, perhaps as a necklace. Each carries some kind of pictorial inscription. The use of these seals began in Mesopotamia and was brought to Anatolia by the Assyrians.

44

There the native people adapted their use and Anatolian artists adopted local scenes for their decoration. The seals show an exquisite, fine workmanship which one can fully appreciate only with the help of a magnifying glass. They served both as an identity card and an amulet. On many of them the name of the owner is inscribed along with a prayer that the god whose form also appears will protect the person. This kind of seal may be what is referred to in the story of Tamar and Judah (Gen. 38:18) when Tamar took Judah's seal as a pledge. The custom of wearing amulets is still observed in Turkey today.

A silver and lead mine at Ak Dağ north of Kanesh was a major source of the main trading medium for the Assyrian merchants who lived on the outskirts of the city. Silver was used throughout the Mediterranean to pay for imported tin which came at first from the Caucasus and the Transcaucasus.

Kanesh may be the capital, known as Nesa, of King Anittas. Nesa was important after Hattusas was destroyed. The town was burnt — hence the present name Kültepe (ash hill) — during a war between two Hittite princes.

GORDIUM — GORDION

Gordium was probably the capital of Meshech. It was located where the Royal Road of Persian Kings crossed the Sangarius (Sakarya) River. Thus it was an active commercial center. A reference to Meshech's trade in slaves and bronze occurs in Ezekiel 27:13. Excavations in the last forty years indicate that it was occupied as early as the third millennium B.C. Between 2000 and 1200 B.C. the city was an important Hittite outpost with Assyrian colonists also living there. (This parallels the situation in Kanesh at the same time.) The city became even more active when Phrygians settled there beginning in the ninth century; it reached its highest prosperity under them in the eighth century. By 690 Cimmerians had invaded the area and destroyed the city. Perhaps Ezekiel was referring to this holocaust when he wrote, "There are Meshech and Tubal with all their hordes, with their buried around them, all of them strengthless and slain by the sword, men who once struck terror into the land of the living" (Ezek. 32:26). Lydians repaired the city, but in 547-546 Cyrus and his army destroyed it again. Under the Persians, however, it regained its place as a commercial and military center. Alexander the Great in 333 cut the famous Gordian knot and took the city out of Persian control, but then in 278 it was destroyed by the Gauls. By 200 A.D. the city was completely deserted.

Seventeenth and sixteenth century Hittite graves have been excavated and some of their contents are to be seen at the Museum of Anatolian Civilizations in Ankara. In Gordium itself there are almost a hundred tumulus graves of notables who lived and died between Phrygian and Galatian times. These stand out above the gently rolling landscape. The largest tumulus has been identified as that belonging to King Midas. It still contains some wooden furniture probably from his palace. (Midas in Assyrian records is a Mushki; in Greek references he is a Phrygian. Perhaps he was both, or maybe they were one and the same.) Most of the finds from the tumuli are in the Ankara museum for safe-keeping. Those include furniture decorated with ivory inlay (from pre-Cimmarian times), wooden statues, vases, bronze cauldrons, silver and gold jewelry, and images of Cybele, the Mother Goddess, used in religious ceremonies. In the Phrygian palaces and public buildings are the earliest examples known in Anatolia of decorative geometric patterns made with colored pebbles. The mosaic technique suggests that the artists may have been familiar with weaving or with basketry.

45

TOGARMAH — GÜRÜN

Togarmah, or Gürün, is one of the many tantalizing examples in the Near East of a place whose name suggests that it or some place close by might be an important archeological site. Ezekiel speaks of Beth-togarmah's army as a northern force which Israel would have to reckon with (Ezek. 38:2). Was there once a fortress here? It lies on the Tohma River, a tributary of the Euphrates, which comes down from the nearby Tahtalı Dağ. At one time it was called Gauraina, and the trade route between Sebasteia (Sivas), and Germaniceia (Maraş) passed through it. But even yet almost nothing is known about its history.

In its recent past Gürün had some reputation for shawls made there. At present it is a town of about 10,000 people whose main activities are in weaving and the grain market. Its public library contains a number of valuable Arabic, Persian, and Ottoman manuscripts.

MT. ARARAT — BÜYÜK AĞRI DAĞI

Mt. Ararat is located in eastern Turkey near the Armenian, Nahcivan and Iranian borders. As the crow flies, it is about 250 kilometers east of Erzurum, 130 kilometers southeast of Kars, and 160 kilometers north of Van. The main road between Turkey and Iran goes from Erzurum through Doğubayazıt (just south of Ararat) to Tabriz. The summit of Mt. Ararat is 5,165 meters above sea level. It is higher than any mountain in the continental United States except for Alaska or in Europe outside the Caucasus.

Ararat is a dormant volcano; the last eruption was on June 2, 1840. At present the upper third of the mountain is covered with snow all the time; the last hundred meters of snow at the top have turned to ice. For climbers on the mountain, fresh running water is available after the sun has been up a while to melt the snow, but it is cut off in the late afternoon when cold air has overcome the heat of the sun. Below the snow the slopes are covered with great blocks of black basalt rock—some as large as village houses.

Over the years various groups have explored Mt. Ararat in

the hopes of finding remains of Noah's ark. Both Josephus in about 70 A.D. and Marco Polo about 1300 A.D. mention its existence on the mountain, but their reports are based on others' accounts. Josephus remarks that its remains are on display for all to see without need of an organized exploration. In more recent years many groups have hunted for it there. The possibility that ancient fables are historical fact is intriguing, and each new discovery of truth in previously discredited records gives additional strength to continuing the search for archeological confirmation.

47

However, the problems of establishing exactly what the biblical record in this case means are serious ones that need to be settled even before one accepts this particular high mountain as the right place to look for the ark. (In itself even that ignores the possibility that Noah and his family used up the ark in bits and pieces to build their new homes—a fate that has destroyed many other famous structures in the Near East since.)

The story of Noah's ark, as it is told in the Bible, is a reworking of an earlier Babylonian myth recorded in the Gilgamesh Epic.* The hero of the earlier version is one Utnapishtim, the favorite of Ea, the god of wisdom. It seems probable that the Babylonian story was based on an unusually devastating flood in the Euphrates River basin, and that the ark in it grounded on the slopes of one of the Zagros mountains. The biblical word that we read as "Ararat" could as well be read "Urartu"; the text has merely "rrt" and the proper vowels must be supplied. Urartu was the name of a historical kingdom, but the word also meant "a land far away" and "a place in the north." So, while Büyük Ağrı Dağı is a spectacular mountain and not a difficult one to climb for those experienced in high altitude exercise, it still seems less than likely that Noah's ark will be found there. That doubt does not detract from the continuing interest in it, nor from the important achievements of archeologists in deepening our understanding of the Old Testament.

*See "The Deluge" in *Ancient Near Eastern Texts,* ed. James B. Pritchard, p. 42 ff. Also *Treasures of the British Museum,* ed. Frank Francis, for pictures of this epic and a cuneiform inscription of the Legend of the Flood, pp. 88-89.

On the north side, Mt. Ararat has its roots in the Araxes (Aras) River valley. There it rises from the valley elevation of about 760 meters above sea level. In that area the Araxes River is the border demarcation between Turkey, Armenia, and Nahcivan. The top of the mountain is only about 30 kilometers from the border. For some years both the Turkish and the other governments have been touchy about foreigners exploring on Ararat because of military security precautions. Therefore it is difficult to get permission to climb it.

If one has that permission, it is best to plan the trip starting from Doğubayazıt on the south, a saving of more than a kilometer in climbing. One can start from Doğubayazıt by jeep or sturdy station wagon, travelling across the valley to the base of the mountain where local guides (who must be engaged beforehand) will meet the party. The average hiker who is experienced in high altitudes can make the climb in three days, but it is better to plan four days to allow for exploration of the top. Late August is the best season.

VAN, TOPRAKKALE

Van was once the center of the Kingdom of Urartu; it was known as Tushpa. It is located on the eastern shore of Lake Van in eastern Turkey. It became the center of an Armenian kingdom founded by Tigranes the Great in the first century B.C. There is a great citadel there which one should visit.

Nearby, in Gevaş which is about thirty-five kilometers southwest of Van, one can hire a boat to the little island of Ahtamar where there are impressive ruins of a tenth century Armenian church. The outside walls of the church are decorated with designs and bas-reliefs of biblical scenes such as Adam and Eve, David and Goliath, and Jonah. A number of other similar Christian churches are in this area.

Two Urartian citadels have been partially excavated in Turkey, the one at Van and the other at nearby Toprakkale. King Ispuinis had a temple to the god Chaldis at his palace on the rock of Van. The oldest building still standing at the foot of this citadel was probably a guard house protecting the water supply. (Although Lake Van covers 3,760 square kilometers, its water is not suitable for drinking or for irrigating. In about 752 King Ispuinis's son Menuas built an aqueduct seventy-five kilometers long to supply the irrigation water for the eastern side of the lake.

Excavations at Toprakkale have revealed details of life in the capital of the Urartian Kings Rusa I and III. Shields and wine jugs from it are on display in the Museum of Anatolian Civilizations in Ankara.

49

SEPHARAD, SARDIS

Sepharad is presumably the same as Sardis, and the Jews who figure in Obadiah 20-21 were probably prisoners of war. Since the date of Obadiah may be either about 450 B.C. or 350 B.C. it is difficult to be sure in which war they were captured, or if it was their parents who had been carried off.

The first settlement in lower Sardis appears to have been about 800 B.C. The city had a colorful history (see Chapter IX), and was an important center well into the Christian era. South of the present highway the excavators found the market place of the Lydian city which was used from about 700 B.C. to 300 B.C. In the shops were many pieces of pottery which have given information about the life of the period.

Another building excavated since 1958 is a third century A.D. Jewish synagogue; its mosaic paving was largely intact when it was uncovered. The building has been partially restored with sparkling white marble. Byzantine shops similar to those in the earlier Lydian market backed up against the wall of the synagogue. One wonders if the synagogue had been built on the site of a more ancient building, or if the owners of the shops could have been distant descendents of the Jews in Obadiah.

TIGRIS AND EUPHRATES RIVERS —
DİCLE AND FIRAT

Both the Tigris and the Euphrates Rivers rise in central

Turkey. The Euphrates has recently been dammed at Keban to provide hydroelectric power for Anatolia. The upper Euphrates consists of two main branches, the more northerly Karasu and the Murat which is longer and carries more water. The earthen Keban Dam was built near the point where these two meet. Near Erzurum the Karasu is separated by only a few kilometers from the Araxes River which flows east to the Caspian Sea. Together the valleys of these two have long made a natural path between northern Persia and the West. The Murat rises in the mountains north of Lake Van. Cuneiform inscriptions have been found in several places along both branches of the river, particularly at Palu and Kale. South of Kale the Euphrates cuts through the Southeast Taurus Mountains in a wild succession of rapids and cataracts. At Keferdiz it runs close to the source of the Tigris at Lake Hazar. In early times it was important as a political boundary: it separated the Assyrian and Hittite Kingdoms; later it was the eastern end of the Roman Empire. At Samosata (Samsat), the capital of the Seleucid kings of Commagene, the Persian Royal Road from Sardis to Susa crossed the river. Birtha (Birecik) was the ford (a bridge was built there in 1953) on the main road from İskenderun (Alexandretta) to Mosul.

The Tigris is a shorter river but in its lower reaches carries a greater volume of water than the Euphrates. Like the Euphrates, it is divided in two main branches, the town of Bitlis near Lake Van being on one, the city of Diyarbakır on the other. There are numerous cuneiform inscriptions and bas-reliefs at points in the cliffs along the western and the eastern branches of the Tigris, and also at its two sources.

Now the Turkish Government is engaged in realizing the Southeastern Anatolia Project, a system of thirteen separate projects (including the Atatürk Dam at Karababa) which will provide hydroelectric power and will irrigate over 4 million acres (1.634 million hectares) of land in the Tigris-Euphrates valleys. All of the provinces of Urfa and Mardin will be affected as well as parts of Gaziantep, Adıyaman, Diyarbakır and Siirt. Again this Mesopotamia -- the Land Between the Rivers -- is becoming green.

OLD TESTAMENT LOCATIONS

EDEN

Traditionally the Garden of Eden has been located in the fertile area between the Tigris and Euphrates Rivers. These rivers both rise in central Turkey; however Eden is usually thought of as being closer to the mouths of the rivers than in the foothills of the Zagros Mountains where some of the earliest archeological remains of civilized man have been found. It is in this area that the Neolithic Revolution took place. One wonders if the story of man's eating the fruit of the tree of knowledge is related to the story of his emergence from instinctive food gatherer to responsible food-producer.

*
* *

Many of the sites in Asia Minor mentioned in the Old Testament are in the eastern or south central part. The writers of the Old Testament naturally had the most contacts with people from the areas closest to them. But often the references were vague, and archeologists today still have difficulty trying to pinpoint places such as Gomer and Tarshish, to say nothing of Ararat.

Some of the non-geographical references of the Bible still echo in the lives of the people today. If a village does not own or have the use of a combine the people heap their grain on a windy threshing-floor to winnow it as in the story of Ruth and Boaz. Abraham's sacrifice of a ram instead of his son is commemorated yearly by Muslims in the Festival of Sacrifice; Muslims believe that the son saved thus was Ishmael, not Isaac. Crops of olives, figs, and grapes are important in the economy of the area and Jotham's fable (Judg. 9:7-15) of the trees that once upon a time decided to anoint a king and could only succeed in persuading the bramble to take the responsibility is a lesson even for people outside the Near East. And, the sense of responsibility to the stranger to take him into one's home is a strong tradition particularly in rural Anatolia where the invitation may be unsophisticated but is always gracious and genuine.

BIBLICAL SITES IN TURKEY

52

With the New Testament many more of the places are well-known than those of the Old Testament and many still show evidences of first and second century Christianity. Also many more written records in known languages exist the closer we come to our own time. The New Testament sites are in western Turkey where the Greco - Roman influence was strong. Perhaps it was because of the Hellenized Jewish communities and their ties with Europe that Christianity became first a predominantly Western religion. Without question the Westernization was also because of the force of Paul's zeal and intellect and his unflinching spirit in proclaiming the Christian message. But one must remember that the New Testament was written in Greek describing the expansion of the church through Greek-speaking areas. There were similar important expansions through Syriac and other areas that it does not record.

CHAPTER IV

ANATOLIA IN THE TIME OF
THE NEW TESTAMENT

The people living in the Asia Minor of the New Testament seem much closer to us today than those of the Old Testament. They attended the theater to see plays that still move us to tears or laughter. They listened to concerts in the odeon, and their government officials struggled with the problems of state as they sat in conference in the bouleuterion. They were religious; perhaps they had a greater respect for the awesomeness of their nature gods than we for the omnipotence of our scientific and material gods. As we today climb over the fallen marbles of these buildings we could do worse than hold in honor the people who built them and the richness they bequeathed to us.

POLITICAL DIVISIONS

Up until the unification of the greater part of Asia Minor under the Roman Empire, the history had been one of a succession of small states that rose and fell in relation to the strength or weakness of the local ruler. Roman control began in 190 B.C. when the Seleucid ruler, Antiochus the Great, was defeated at Magnesia. The control spread in 133 B.C. when the first Roman province, Asia, was organized in the region around Ephesus. Bithynia, Pontus, and Cilicia next came under Roman rule and shortly before the Christian era began Galatia and Cappadocia were added. The period of the early development of Christianity was one of peace and stability throughout this area. This undoubtedly influenced the speed with which the new religion spread.

After the reorganization of the Roman Empire by Diocletian in 297 A.D. the area was again split into small political units which eventually became part of the Byzantine Empire. Christianity, which spread north and west from Antioch and along the historic trade routes, caused major changes by providing a common language and religion for the whole country.

For most of the purposes of this book these area names are important mainly to help identify which particular city is being discussed: Antioch of Pisidia and Antioch-on the-Orontes, Seleucia Pieria and Seleucia of Isauria. The maps at the beginning of the book should also be helpful in locating the areas and the cities.

SOUTHERN COAST

Cilicia

South of the Taurus Mountains lies the fertile plain of Cilicia known today as Çukurova. The main entrances to the plain from the central highland were either down the Calycadnus (Göksu) River or through the Cilician Gates, a narrow rock pass on the Cydnus (Tarsus Suyu) River through which many armies including Alexander's have filed. One of the district's main exports in Roman times was cilicum, the goat's-hair cloth from which tents were made. Other important exports were oil and pine wood for timber. Towns and cities included Claudiopolis (Mut), Danunas (Adana), and Alexandretta (İskenderun).

Pamphylia

The narrow coastal area between the Taurus Mountains and the northern extent of the Mediterranean Sea is the district of Pamphylia. Side, Perga, Aspendos, and Attalia (Antalya) are among the cities important in antiquity; Antalya is still an important port.

Lycia

The area now designated as the Antalya province is the general center of classical Lycia. Milas was included by some writers in the district, but the more important cities seem to have been Patara (Gelemiş) in the Xanthus Valley, Telmessus (Fethiye), and Myra (Demre). Perhaps it is Lycians who are mentioned in an Egyptian account of the Hittite battle at Qadesh. They may also be the Luqqa in the Hittite documents of the fourteenth and thirteenth centuries B.C.

INTERIOR

Commagene

55

Between the Taurus Mountains and the Euphrates River was the district of Commagene, the farthest northeastern part of ancient Syria. The Assyrian general, Sargon II, who waged a number of wars from 722 to 705 B.C., was one of its early kings. Commagene was about the last of his triumphs; previously he had fought and defeated among others the Samarians, the Philistines, the' Egyptians, the Babylonians, the people of Urartu, the Hittites, the people of Meshech, and the Minrli. In more recent times its kings were affiliated with the Seleucids. About 30 B.C. Antiochus I of Commagene decided to make a place of worship that would immortalize himself. Thus he started a temple and a necropolis on Mt. Nimrud (Nemrut Dağı, east of Adıyaman) which were embellished with mammoth statues to twenty-five kings, gods, lions, and eagles. Through the ravages of weather and earthquakes these statues have come to present a macabre scene of bodyless stone heads. For a while Commagene was a Roman province. The satirist, Lucian, was born there in 120 A.D. In Byzantine times it was a center of Syrian culture.

Cappadocia

The central plateau of Asia Minor north of the Taurus Mountains and east of the central salt desert of Axylon (Cihanbeyli Yaylası and Tuz Gölü) was the stronghold of the early Hittite empire. Mt. Argaeus (Erciyes Dağı) towers to 3,916 meters over the plain with Caesarea Mazaca (Kayseri) being the capital of the kingdom. The striking features of the landscape have been caused by the volcanic activity of Mt. Argaeus and the several other volcanoes of the area and the subsequent erosion. Argaeus last erupted in ancient times. A large Armenean population was located in the east and northeastern parts from 70 A.D. on. Some of the Persians who settled there after the sixth century B.C. introduced the fire worship of Zoroaster. The Iranian influence continued strong at least until Cappadocia became a Roman province in the first century B.C.

56

Galatia

The name of the area, settled by Celtic tribes (Gauls) in the third century B.C. has reference to the upland area of Asia Minor around Ankara. It became a part of the Roman Empire under Augustus in 25 B.C. When Paul was travelling through the area the government and commercial language was Greek, though in the towns of Ancyra (Ankara), Tavium, and Pessinus (Ballıhisar) the local Celtic language was more popular. These three were the capitals of three Celtic tribes, the Tectosages, the Tolistobogii, and the Trocmi. There is a possibility that when Paul wrote his Letter to the Galatians the people he was concerned with lived in the southern part of the Roman province between Konya and Antalya rather than around Ankara.

Isauria - Lycaonia

The boundaries of this district varied greatly at different periods of history. In general it lay in the watershed of the Calycadnus (Göksu) River. As late as the fourth century A.D. the people of both Isauria and Cilicia were well known as pirates.

Pisidia

In ancient geography this was the mountainous area north of Antalya with two fair-sized lakes, Karalis (Beyşehir Gölü) and Limnai (Eğridir Gölü). Termessus in the south, Sagalassus (Ağlasun) to the north, and Antioch of Pisidia (Yalvaç) are some of the early important towns.

Phrygia

The extensive western part of central Anatolia, the boundaries of which varied greatly over the years, is the area of Phrygia. The people seem to have been widely spread throughout the Aegean region also. Greek tradition has it that the Bryges are the oldest of all people and their language the original tongue; however they now appear to have supplanted an older civilization, possibly the Mushki, enemies of the Hittites. Among their kings are Midas of the golden touch and Gordius of the knot, whose kingdoms were in the Sangarius (Sakarya) River valley. The larger cities were Dorylaeum (Eskişehir), Cotyaeum (Kütahya) and Trajanopolis (Uşak), with Laodicea and Colossae also included. Phrygians are credited with having invented the frieze.

57

AEGEAN COAST

Caria

Caria is a mountainous area along the southwestern Aegean coast of Turkey. Cnidus (now an archeological site), Halicarnassus (Bodrum, birthplace of Herodotus, c. 490 B.C. and famous for the monument to King Mausolus), Miletus, Priene, and Magnesia are the main cities of ancient times. The most important bay, the Ceramic Gulf or the Gulf of Cos (Kerme Körfezi), has always been feared by sailors for the treachery of its winds, and today is proving a rich source for underwater archeology because of the numerous shipwrecks. Caria extended inland as far as the city of Aphrodisias (Geyre), a place famous then for medicine, philosophy, and sculpture. People now marvel at the size of its stadium.

Asia

While the term Asia originally seems to have meant east of the rising sun, it was used by Greek historians to refer specifically to the area around Ephesus (Efes) where the Ionians first settled. The Hittite's word for the area was Assuwa. Their use of the word to mean the East is one of the evidences that they arrived in Anatolia from the West, not from the south or from Ararat. Another possibility would be that Assuwa looked like the land they had known as children and they called it the same name out of homesickness. In Egyptian hieroglyphics the word *Isij* (probably the same word) meant also good or fortunate.

Besides Ephesus which was the capital, Pergamum (Bergama), Miletus (Milet), Sardis (Sart), and Smyrna (İzmir) were also at times a part of the province and were centers of culture and education.

58

Lydia

Sardis was the capital of Lydia. The district boundaries changed at different times, but in general the land was that of the present provinces of İzmir and Manisa. According to Herodotus, Lydus, the founder, was the brother of Mysus (Mysia) and Car (Caria). Herodotus also says that the Lydians were the first to strike and use gold and silver coins. The Lydians were known to Jeremiah (46:9) as mercenaries in the Egyptian army. Lydian inscriptions of about the sixth century B.C. concern mercenaries in the Egyptian army and support the biblical record.*

Mysia

The area south and west of the Sea of Marmara and the Dardanelles is the general district of Mysia with Pergamum (Bergama) and Cyzicus (Erdek) the main cities. Mysians are among those named by Homer as allies of Troy.

Troas

The northwestern promontory of Asia Minor around Troy is the area of Troas or the Troad. Its southeastern border is Mt. Ida (Kaz Dağı). The chief Greek towns were Ilium or Troy, Assos, and Alexandria Troas, now all in ruins. Troas is often included in the area of Mysia.

---

* See Friedrich, **Kleinasiatische Sprachdenkmäler,** p. 122.

NEW TESTAMENT ANATOLIA

BLACK SEA

Bithynia

The Bithyni were a tribe that migrated from Thrace to Asia Minor and gave their name to the southwest shores of the Black Sea, the Bosphorus, and the Sea of Marmara. The most important mountain of the area is Mt. Olympus, known now as Ulu Dağ; the cities were Prusa (Bursa) at the foot of Mt. Olympus, Nicomedia (İzmit), Nicaea (İznik), and Chalcedon (Kadıköy). The land was well wooded and fertile.

Paphlagonia

The Paphlagonians were among the oldest peoples of Asia according to early historians. The region included the triangle of land around Sinope (Sinop), Gangra (Çankırı), and Amastris (Amasra) bordering the Black Sea. One of their early leaders was Pylaemenes, the leader of the Paphlagonians in Homer's *Iliad*.

Pontus

At its greatest extent Pontus included the Black Sea coast from just west of Amisus (Samsun) to the present Soviet border with the high mountainous regions and table lands extending inland as far as Sebasteia (Sivas). The first capital of the Persian dynasty in the area was at Amasia (Amasya) where there are still rock tombs of four kings. In the New Testament the references to Pontus were to the people in the western part whose attitudes were Roman. Pontus was the land of the Amazons and the home of Strabo who praised the coastal region from Trapezus (Trabzon) west for its productiveness and scenic beauty.

EUROPE

Thrace

At the time that Thrace was a Roman province it comprised the land north of the Dardanelles, the Sea of Marmara, and the Bosphorus to the Balkan Mountains and the Nestus River. All of what is presently European Turkey was then Thrace; it also included southern Bulgaria and northeastern Greece. The most important of all the cities of Thrace then were Heraclea Perinthus (Marmara Ereğlisi) and later Byzantium (Istanbul). The early Thracians and Dardanii (famous in the Trojan story) were always tattooed and were noted for their skill in music and literature. According to Greek mythology, Orpheus, who charmed even the rocks and trees when he sang and played his lyre, was born on the Hermus (Meriç) River in Thrace. Sepulchral mounds from the prehistoric period still mark the Thracian landscape.

60

PAGAN RELIGIONS

At the beginning of Christianity most of the people in Asia Minor were worshippers of one or more of the local gods known today mostly through Greek and Roman mythology. (There also were Jewish settlements throughout the area.) Rites at the temples to the gods attracted their devotees and initiates from some distance away. The Greek traveller and geographer of the second century A.D., Pausanias, has left a description of some of the details of the ceremonies and superstitious customs of his time. Earlier accounts are to be found in Homer and Hesiod. Other information has had to be pieced together from bas-reliefs, meager contemporary references, or literature of a much later period.

Among the many gods and goddesses who were worshipped at this time were Zeus, Poseidon, Artemis, Pan, Dionysus, Apollo, Athena, Aphrodite, Cybele, and Mithra. Much fuller descriptions of these can be found in other sources; however a few words about each may help give something of the background of the early church's concerns about rival religions. But one needs to be reminded today that when Christianity started, and for several hundred years thereafter, it attracted a relatively very small group of people. Probably most of the people then as now were more concerned with their worldly affairs than their spiritual, and were content to accept the current conventions without much questioning.

CYBELE

Cybele, the Great Mother of the Gods, is one of the deities native to Asia Minor. Her worship goes back at least to the Hittite mother-figure, Kubaba, in Hittite scenes. Her cult centered in Phrygia, but she was worshipped throughout Anatolia as the nature deity, and hers was one of the last of the pagan cults to die out. Her annual festival first came on April 4, but then moved up into March during the time of the Roman Empire. Cybele was usually worshipped along with Attis, the god of vegetation, and the climax of their celebrations coincided with the return of spring. Along with other mystery religions the cult of Cybele was both a rival of Christianity and a stimulus in its development.

MITHRA

Mithra,* the Persian god of air, light, loyalty, and truth, was worshipped throughout the Roman Empire. His cult was the greatest threat to Christianity by the fourth century, particularly as belief in it was strong among the army and commercial groups in Rome when Christianity was threatening the established customs of the state. Its beginnings go back long before the fall of the Persian Empire. Mithraism bound its members in close fraternal fellowship, wiping out distinctions between rich and poor, slave and senator. Mithra, who was identified with the sun, was the mediator between suffering humanity and the unattainable supreme god, Ormuzd. Mithraism was both a popular religion and a "mystery," a cult with secret rites and a ceremony of initiation. Many of its secrets seem to have been lost.

It is unlikely that there was any significant influence by Mithraism on early Christianity in Asia Minor. However, a number of similarities between this cult and Christianity are striking, and suggest that there may have been some borrowing between them or from a common source: the marvel of the birth of Mithra was seen only by shepherds who came to bring gifts and adore him; the birth of the Sun was celebrated on December 25th; the initiates were

* Variant spellings include Mitra and Mithras.

expected to maintain a high moral rectitude, and they looked forward to a better life after death. They believed in the immortality of the soul and resurrection after death. Those entering one of the top degrees of the mystery (there were seven stages) took part in a symbolic banquet like the Christian communion. The main differences were that Mithraism sought to accommodate itself to Roman polytheism (thus it was not in collision with the state) while Christianity was decidedly monotheistic. Mithraism was based on a mythical rather than a historical person; and it admitted no women to its privileges.

ARTEMİS

Artemis (the Roman Diana) was the goddess of chastity. Her worship at Ephesus was influenced both by Greek athletic and Eastern orgiastic rites, and there she was also connected with the Amazons. The chief festival was held in the spring. Second century A.D. representations of her as a female with many breasts may be seen in the museums in Selçuk and İzmir among other places.

APHRODITE

Aphrodite, the goddess of love, beauty, and fertility, is Eastern in origin; she is the Assyrian Ishtar and the Persian Astarte. Among her symbols are the moon, a ram (fertility) and the cypress, myrtle, and pomegranates (remedies against sterility). The most famous of her statues was the one sculpted by Praxiteles for the city of Cnidus. Aphrodisias in Caria was one of the best known cities named after her.

APOLLO

Apollo was the god of prophecy and of agriculture; he was both a warlike god and a healing god. Three of his oracles on the Aegean Coast of Asia Minor were important: one at Claros (near Ephesus), one at Patara, and one at Didyma.

ATHENA

Athena, protectress of cities and goddess of war, was also goddess of wisdom and of crafts. Her main temple was the Parthenon in Athens.

POSEIDON

Poseidon, god of the sea, was believed to cause earthquakes and storms at sea, to support the earth, and to be the god of springs. Black bulls, representing the stormy sea, were sacrificed to him. His main temple was at Mycale where the Ionian national festival, the Panionia, was held.

63

PAN

Pan in Phrygia was known as Marsyas. He was a river god who played the flute so well that he challenged Apollo to a musical contest. King Midas took his side and received the punishment of donkey's ears for his trouble. Marsyas was turned into the Meander River which begins near the present city of Dinar.

DIONYSUS

The worship of Dionysus, the god of wine, was strong in Phrygia and Lydia. His Lydian name was Bacchus. Here he was associated with Cybele, and his bacchanalian procession included centaurs and satyrs in his train. He taught people how to grow grapes. Because he was associated with farming and the first stages of civilization he was thought of as a lawgiver. The people representing satyrs wore goat skins in the rites. One theory is that as they danced and sang they pretended to be something they were not. Their dialogues or "goat songs" (in Greek: *tragos* — goat plus *oide* — song) thus may have been the first tragedies.

ZEUS

Zeus, the father of the gods, was preeminent among the gods long before Homer described the beliefs about him. The earliest rituals associated with him involve human sacrifice, an event present in the worship of many other dieties. The later development of the ideas of his political and moral character strongly influenced Greek civilization and its contributions to Western thought.

It is difficult from this distance in time to weigh the influence of the pagan cults on the direction of the development of early Christianity. It is unlikely that Jesus or his immediate group knew much or cared about the nature gods. No evidence of that exists in the Gospels although Judaism inveighed constantly against polytheism. Cer tainly as the church moved north and west and began to include Gentiles in its membership there was a much deeper contact with paganism and a threat from its attractions. But the basic difference between Christianity and paganism remained: Jesus was a real man, an historical person and not a myth, through whom by the grace of God — not by one's deserving — all could be saved.

JUDAISM

While the Jews were a minority people in Asia Minor, there were groups of them living in most of the cities and probably there they were numerous and powerful enough to exert an influence in trade, finance, and government. Remains of large Jewish synagogues are still to be seen in places like Sardis. The Jewish population in Turkey today, however, does not trace its residence back to pre-Christian times but rather to the time of the Spanish Inquisition at the end of the fifteenth century when Spanish Jews were given refuge in the Ottoman Empire.

In most of the Hellenic cities the Jewish population at the time of the New Testament did not have any rights as citizens but rather were resident aliens. However, Roman citizenship was given to those who rendered a notable service to the state. Paul inherited his citizenship from his father, so perhaps one of his ancestors had been granted citizenship rights. There probably was a well-established Jewish community in Tarsus in Paul's time.

Jewish settlements at Tarsus and other places had been started as a part of Seleucid practice in the reconstruction of cities in Cilicia, Lydia, and Phrygia in the middle of the second century B.C. One of the intents of the Seleucid kings was to raise the level of civilization and to unify all the people under their control by a broad study of Greek language and ideas. This they attempted to enforce on the Jews and thereby provoked the Maccabean revolt (222 to 135 B.C.), the aim of which was to protect the uniqueness of Judaism against the Hellenistic threat.

65

EDUCATION — CULTURE

Many of the remains of classical antiquity are evidence of the importance the peoples then gave to culture. Buildings such as theaters, odeons, and libraries, mosaics, frescoes, and statues, jewelry, plays, odes and epics, and even the common household vases and mirrors from that time have the enduring quality of great art.

There were famous schools and what we might call research centers throughout the area: the Asclepieum at Pergamum (Bergama) was a medical institute; there was also an important school of sculpture there. Tarsus was a university town, a center of culture, and Strabo praises its people for their general education and eagerness for philosophy.

The library in Pergamum was so famous that it attracted the jealousy of Ptolemy. He forbad the export of papyrus so that the number of books there would be limited, Instead, the kings of Pergamum developed the use of skins — parchment — and unwittingly caused papyrus to be outmoded. Parchment did not roll or fold as well as papyrus and so the codex or paged book came to be used. This library was given by Anthony to Cleopatra, and then was destroyed in the seventh century A.D. by the Caliph Omar.

According to the inscriptions on either side of the front steps of the library buildings in Ephesus, Consul Gaius Julius Aquila erected the Celsus library in 100 A.D. for his father, Gaius Julius Celsus Polemaeanus. That scholar has been able to remain in his library: he was buried in a lead casket enclosed in a marble sarcophagus that is still underneath the building.

While the art forms of music and dance have not left as many tangible traces as the theater and plastic arts, there are many references to them in the literature and the paintings of the period. Scenes of people playing harps, lutes, and pipes are fairly common on the decorated vases, and no classical Greek play is complete without its singing dance intervals of strophes and antistrophes.

THE UNION OF EAST AND WEST

As has always been true, the land of Asia Minor has acted as a bridge for people to carry the developments in ideas from their point of origin to their places of modification, application, and proliferation. Often it has been the many insights of the past that people have gathered, blended together, and thereby used to create something new and revolutionary. This is in large measure Paul's contribution to Christian theology: an amalgamation of Hebrew and Near Eastern thought.

As Ramsay says in *The Cities of St. Paul,*

> [Paul] appreciated well, and declared emphatically that the old system had an element of good; but without fundamental reform it could not be preserved. The Hellenistic kingdoms of the East struck out [coined] many admirable devices in society and in administration, or else borrowed them from the older Oriental States and improved them as they took them; the Roman Empire appropriated many of these devices and wrought them into its own vast system of government; but neither in Hellenistic nor in Roman times did these admirable devices rest on a broad enough and safe enough basis.

In the philosophy of Paul, the Eastern mind and the Hellenic have been intermingled in the closest union, like two elements which have undergone a chemical mixture...

...In fully conscious thought during his maturer years he broadened both Judaism and Hellenism till they were co-extensive with the world and co-incident with one another.*

The pilgrimage that today's travellers in Asia Minor are on is often a search for that which makes this land holy. They may find hints of it in the ruined buildings, in the relics of the bones of saints, or in colorful anemones, the lilies of the fields which gypsies sell on the street corners in January. Certainly there is a human need to deepen one's faith by means of outside stimuli of many kinds. It is to be hoped that the pilgrim-tourists will be able to feel an increased awareness of the reality and richness of the religious experience of the early followers of Jesus through seeing the real places those people also travelled. Perhaps one might even hope for a modern "harmony" of East and West to grow out of this awareness.

CHAPTER V

TURKEY'S
SOUTHEASTERN COAST

SELECTED REFERENCES:

Antioch: Acts 6:5; 11:19-30; 13:1-3; 15:1-2, 22-35
Seleucia Pieria: Acts 13:4
Tarsus: Acts 9:11, 30; 11:25; 21:39; 22:3, 25-29

ANTIOCH-ON-THE-ORONTES — ANTAKYA

It is appropriate to begin the description of the biblical sites of the New Testament with Antioch, the most southern of those in Turkey, because this is where the followers of Jesus were first called Christians. After the stoning of Stephen for blasphemy in Jerusalem (Acts 7) in about 33 or 34 A.D., the fairly sizeable Jerusalem congregation of the followers of Jesus dispersed, and many of the people returned to their native cities. Nicholas of Antioch, a convert to Judaism and one of the "seven men of good reputation" (Acts 6:3-5) appointed to take charge of the practical arrangements of the bilingual communal body of believers, may well have been one of those. With the addition to the Antioch community of many who were not Jewish, a distinguishing name was needed, and so the new word, Christian, came into use, perhaps about 40 A.D.

Antioch had been refounded and named by one of Alexander the Great's generals, Seleucus Nicator, who obtained this area (along with a great deal more) after the Battle of Ipsus in 301 B.C. He named the city for his father, Antiochus. The capture of the land around Antioch had been one of the steps in Alexander's grand strategy of uniting Europe and Asia into one Hellenic civilization under one ruler. As Antioch lay on the Orontes (Âsi) River and on the main road between Asia Minor and the lands to the south, Seleucus Nicator was here in a excellent position from which he could further that Hellenization which Alexander had envisioned. Antioch thus was his capital of the kingdom of Syria.

By the time of Paul, Peter and Barnabas, Antioch had long been an important city. There was a large Jewish community in good standing in the city, and in some of the synagogues the people used the Greek language in their services, reading from the Septuagint. The size of the capital and the use of Greek in the Sabbath service suggest that the people in Antioch were not as conservative as those in the church in Jerusalem. This is part of the reason why it was from Antioch rather than from Jerusalem that Christianity spread out to the world.

In the pre-Christian era there were the beginnings in Antioch of a Gentile community attracted and influenced by the high ethical and spiritual Jewish conception of God and by the code of morals of the worshippers. But even before Paul and Barnabas began preaching to them, a precedent of association between Jews and Gentiles had been set in Samaria: the Roman centurion Cornelius, his relatives, and his close friends who had gathered with him in Caesarea to meet and to listen to Peter had been so moved that they began speaking in tongues of ecstasy and were baptised into the faith (Acts 10). Peter had been prompted to speak with them because of a vision he had seen; in contravention of his Jewish religion he had visited these people of another race. With his recital of the outcome of his visit the members of the church in Judaea accepted that ecstasy as evidence of the baptism of the Holy Spirit. Out of this developed one of the decisive changes in history, the beginning of the universal church. Jesus of Nazareth was no longer the savior of Orthodox or Hellenized Jews alone, he was the Savior of all people.

In connection with this inclusion of outsiders, in Antioch a fierce dispute arose over whether "those who were not circumcised in accordance with Mosaic practice could... be saved." (Acts 15:1). Paul and Barnabas took the liberal point of view; some visitors who had recently come from Judaea argued strongly against it, and to settle

70

the argument Paul and Barnabas were sent to Jerusalem to put their case before the apostles and elders there. Paul and Barnabas told the assembly about the miracles that had been happening in Asia Minor. After Peter and James advised accepting the gift of the Holy Spirit rather than circumcision as proof of God's choice, two representatives, Judas and Silas, were sent back with Paul and Barnabas to deliver a letter welcoming the Gentiles in Antioch, Syria, and Cilicia into the Christian fellowship.

It was from the church in Antioch that Paul and Barnabas set out on their first journey and to which Paul returned at the end of it and of his second journey. Although Tarsus was Paul's family home, Antioch became his home base for his missionary work.

A grotto at the foot of the hills a bit east of the city is known as St. Peter's Grotto. It was discovered by Crusaders and is reputed to be the cave church where early Christians met in secret. A narrow tunnel winds from the church through the side of the hill and away from the town. Presumably it was an escape route. Other early Christian buildings can also be found in Antioch and along the Orontes River toward the sea. The museum in Antioch houses an unusually rich collection of mosaics from the area.

The later history of Antioch parallels the history of the area; between 252 and 300 A.D. ten assemblies of the church were held there, and it became the residence of the Patriarch of Asia. St. Jerome, the one who later prepared the Vulgate, believed he saw Jesus in a vision when he was in Antioch in 373 A.D. The saint most associated with the area was Simeon Stylites, one of a number of ascetics who removed themselves from the world by perching on a column. Simeon Stylites gathered around himself a monastic settlement on a hill about forty miles east of Antioch in what is now Syria; on his death in 459 A.D. he was buried in Antioch. The area was devastated by earthquake and thousands of people were killed in 526 just when a large group of Christians had gathered in Antioch for a church meeting. Two more bad earthquakes occurred soon thereafter. Crusaders held the city from 1098 to 1268. Since then, except for a few years between the two world wars, it has been Turkish.

Two of the bishops of Antioch are famous in church history; Peter is supposed to have been the first. Ignatius was the "second successor of Peter" according to Eusebius. His letters, among them one to Polycarp, are among the earliest pieces of Christian literature we possess. He is strong in placing his belief in the supremacy of Christ above any other basis, including the Old Testament, for faith. Ignatius is supposed to have died a martyr to Christianity in Rome in about 110 A.D.

72

St. John Chrysostom, the fearless, outspoken Patriarch of Constantinople (398-404) was born in Antioch in 345 (?) and got his early training there.

SELEUCIA PIERIA — SAMANDAĞ

The seaport of Antioch in Roman times was at Seleucia. This town was one of many cities founded by and named for Seleucus Nicator. It was located at the mouth of the Orontes River on rocks which form a cliff above the Mediterranean at the foot of Mt. Pieria (Musa Dağı). There were the ruins of a fort here in 300 B.C.; the place has returned to ruins now. İskenderun is presently the main port for Antioch.

Seleucus Nicator was a distinguished officer under Philip of Macedon. He accompanied Alexander the Great on the Asian expedition and became the founder of the Seleucid dynasty that ruled Syria from 312 B.C. until the Roman conquest in 64 B.C. At the height of his power his territory extended from the Oxus and Indus Rivers through all of Syria to the Mediterranean. He reigned thirty-two years from 312 to 280 B.C. when he was murdered in Lysimachia in Thrace at the age of seventy-seven by the son of his friend and ally, Ptolemy. He was an energetic, persevering ruler, founding centers of Greek civilization and culture in almost every province he ruled.

Seleucia is mentioned in the New Testament only as the port from which Paul and Barnabas set sail for Cyprus on their first missionary journey (Acts 13:4).

TARSUS

Tarsus was the home of the young Paul who was born there about the time Jesus was born in Bethlehem. The city had been in existence some 4,000 years before him. It was one of the important towns of the Hittites in the second millennium B.C. and may have been the capital of the Hittite state of Kizzuwatna. When founded it was a seaport; the harbor was a large lagoon opening on the Mediterranean. That lagoon has silted up gradually through the centuries; by the fifth century A.D. it was an impassable swamp. The city is now about fifteen kilometers from the sea and in the midst of rich farm land.

73

The Cydnus (Tarsus Suyu) River flows just east of the city and has played its part in the history of the city. Alexander the Great nearly drowned in its cold waters in 333 B.C. Cleopatra, arrayed as Venus reclining on her throne, arrived in the city in 41 B.C. being rowed by her slaves up the Cydnus on a gaily decorated barge. The purpose of her display was a meeting with "the triple pillar of the world," Mark Anthony, whom she "transformed into a strumpet's fool."*

Several other famous people have been associated with the city. It was captured and sacked by Sennacherib in 696 B.C. A large rectangular cement-like enclosure near the center of town has been labeled, probably falsely, as the tomb of his grandson, Ashurbanipal or Sardanapalus; it may have been a temple to Tarz for whom the city was named. Cicero, the great Roman orator, was governor of Cilicia and lived in Tarsus in 50 B.C. Julius Caesar met representatives of the province in the city in 47 B.C. Mark Anthony exempted Tarsus from taxes when he was there in 41 B.C. because of its resistance to Cassius.

But of all the great men and women who honored Tarsus by their presence none compares with the Apostle Paul in his influence on Christianity. Born a Jew, but, unlike most Jews, having the benefits of Roman citizenship, he attended school in the large Jewish

*Shakespeare, **Anthony and Cleopatra,** Act I, Sc. i, LL, 12-13.

community in Tarsus and learned a trade like all Jewish boys. For him the trade was tent-making, one of the specialties of Tarsus. He must have grown up knowing Aramaic, Hebrew, Greek, Latin and possibly something of the local dialect, too. As a young man he went to Jerusalem to study under the great teacher Gamaliel. He belonged to the Pharisees who held both scripture and tradition to be valid and binding. While in Jerusalem, he was an accomplice in the stoning of Stephen, the first Christian martyr. After his sudden conversion to Christianity on the Damascus road he was active in proclaiming Jesus as the Messiah both there and in Jerusalem. In both cities he aroused so much hatred among the Jews that he had to flee for his life, once escaping to Tarsus.

In the meantime some of the Jerusalem community that had fled because of the repercussions following the death of Stephen had gone to Antioch. There they began speaking to Gentiles. Word of this got back to Jerusalem, and the church there sent Barnabas to investigate. He was favorably impressed, decided he needed someone to help him, and went up to Tarsus to get Paul. This is the last reference to Paul's being in Tarsus in the Bible, but Paul probably went through Tarsus on his second and third missionary journeys before he started up into Galatia and Phrygia.

Tarsus as Paul's birthplace and early home offered an unusually good schooling for the man who would "westernize" Christianity. Tarsus was a meeting place between East and West. Politically it had been part of the Persian Empire and was an eastern port. Later under the Seleucids it was associated with Syria and that mixture of oriental and Hellenistic cultures. As an important commercial center and seaport, Tarsus's entire history was one of mixing East and West. With this blend of cultural environment, it is no wonder that Paul was able to bring together Jew and Gentile into one church and know the strengths and weaknesses of both.

One feels a bit of Paul's pride in his city when he speaks to the commandant of the garrison in Jerusalem in Greek and says, "I am a Jew, a Tarsian from Cilicia, a citizen of no mean city." The commandant seems to have thought he was someone quite different: "You are not the Egyptian who started a revolt some time ago?" he asks with surprise. There must have been a forcefulness in Paul's bearing that gave credence to his claim; even after the commandant said, "it cost me a large sum to acquire this citizenship," Paul answered, "But it was mine by birth," and his word was accepted (Acts 21:39, 22:28).

Paul and Barnabas were so successful in Antioch that they were chosen by the church there to take the Gospel to the lands of the Gentiles. Thus from about the year 47 A.D. to 57 A.D. when he returned from Miletus to Jerusalem, Paul, with one or two other leaders of the church, went through what is now Turkey on his three great missionary journeys. He was arrested in Jerusalem for causing a riot in 57 A.D. Being a Roman citizen he appealed to Caesar for judgment since he thought he could not get an unprejudiced hearing where the riot had occurred. So he was sent to Rome in 58 A.D. According to tradition he was beheaded in 62 or 64 A.D. after the great fire in the reign of Nero.

75

Very little remains in Tarsus today of the city which Paul knew. A gate left from the walled city of the Roman period is now known affectionately as St. Paul's or Cleopatra's Gate. As a tourist attraction it has recently been much restored. While some of the rubble in the construction is possibly from buildings standing in Paul's time, it is unlikely that the gate itself would have been familiar to him. A section of a main street leading to the hippodrome has been uncovered. The foundations of that hippodrome lie under the campus of the Tarsus American College. Catercorner from that school and on the slope of the playground of a primary school is the bank of seats left from the Roman odeon.

Some of the projections on the front side of Ulu Cami are remains of a church; one of them is identified without other explanation as the tomb of "Seth, son of Adam." Eski,

or Kilise, Cami was originally an Armenian church; it has been converted into a mosque. There were three church councils in Tarsun
in 431, 435, and 1177, but there is no church building in use as such
now.

In the hills north of Tarsus is a Cave of the Seven Sleeper (known
in Turkish as Eshabıkehf); a place of pilgrimage, it probably pre-
dates the Christian era. (The Seven Sleepers are also identified
with some ruins in Ephesus.)

SELEUCIA OF ISAURIA — SİLİFKE

About 100 kilometers west of Tarsus is Seleucia bf Isauria. St.
Thecla is said to have been buried in the cemetary near the ruined
basilica in the nearby hill of Meremlik or Ayatekla just south of
Silifke. The church was probably of fifth century construction.
According to *The Acts of Paul and Thecla* written in the second century A.D., St. Thecla was one of those who met Paul first at Iconium.
She set up a nunnery just outside of Seleucia and was so effective
in performing miraculous cures that the doctors of the town lost all
their practice.

The entire Çukurova countryside is dotted with places of interest
to historians, archaeologists, artists, and students of early
Christianity, in addition to those mentioned above which have a
direct connection with the New Testament. During the Third
Crusade Frederick Barbarossa fell off his horse and drowned in the
Calycadnus (Göksu) at Silifke; the Girl's Castle (Kız Kalesi), built by
Armenian kings in the twelfth century, is on an island visible from
the road between Silifke and Mersin. A few columns are left of the
ruins of Soli, a city that used such corrupt Greek that even today
when a person makes an error in grammar it is called a solecism.
Soli was later rebuilt by Pompey and named Pompeiopolis.

CHAPTER VI

CENTRAL TURKEY

SELECTED REFERENCES:

Phrygia, Galatia: Acts 16:6; 18:23
Antioch of Pisidia: Acts 13:14-52; II Timothy 3:11
Iconium: Acts 13:51; 14:1-6, 19; 16:2; II Timothy 3:11
Lystra: Acts 14:6-23; 16:1-4; II Timothy 3:11
Derbe: Acts 14:6, 20-21; 16:1; 20:4

There were two main military roads that went through Cappadocia and crossed at Soandus (Nevşehir) during the Roman period. One linked Ancyra and Tarsus through the Cilician Gates and present-day Niğde. The other linked Iconium and Caesarea Mazaca. This road also continued to Pessinus and Laodicea. But in spite of the main roads, people living here have always felt cut off. The security of the area, the fantastically eroded valleys, and the relative fertility made it a natural refuge from government and religious persecution and encouraged an emphasis on other-worldly contemplation.

CAESAREA MAZACA — KAYSERİ

There is doubt about whether Paul actually visited Caesarea Mazaca, and for that matter Tavium, Ancyra, or Pessinus either. The towns are not named in the New Testament but are included in some of the books about Paul's journeys on the strength of the reference to his journeys through Galatia and on to Phrygia. These towns were important at the time, but it seems more likely that his visits were to the places named in the southern part of Galatia such as Iconium, Lystra, and Derbe.

However, Caesarea Mazaca was an early Christian center. Basil, Bishop of Caesarea from 329 to 379 A.D., was one of the outstanding early church leaders. A scholar, a philanthropist, a reformer, and a man of practical sense and spiritual insight, he interpreted the Christian message with a force and directness that continues to influence the church today. St. Basil is credited with having built a church and monastery north of the city where the poor and sick were cared for. During the sixth century Justinian rebuilt the city walls, most of which are still standing. By the eleventh century there was a large Armenian colony settled nearby.

ÜRGÜP, GÖREME

About 90 kilometers southwest of Kayseri are the unusual towns of Ürgüp, Göreme, Avcılar, Ortahisar, and Üç Hisar with their troglodyte dwellings. Remains of early churches can be seen, complicated rooms hollowed out of the cones of volcanic ash. Several hundred churches are in this area, some of which are decorated with scratched frescoes depicting scenes from the Bible or the Apocrypha. Many of them reflect both the architects' familiarity with conventional Byzantine buildings and their own slavish dependence on that style: false columns and vaulting have been carved into the tuff although the rock was suitable to a more plastic form. The intent then was to recall for the residents their associations with freestanding sanctuaries and the symbolism of the cross and the heavenly dome. For us today the columns that now hang and the arches that end in midair create also a sense of the illusive and the lavish along with their witness to the ravages of time.

This area was most highly populated during the eighth and ninth centuries though there were probably Christians living here from the first century on.

In the valley of the Melendiz Suyu between Aksaray and Ihlara there are more than twenty similar churches with paintings from the ninth to the eleventh centuries. One in Kokar Kilise, Ihlara, shows two shepherds playing instruments that look much like the *ney* (bamboo flute) used today in dervish religious music.

CENTRAL TURKEY

DERİNKUYU, KAYMAKLI

Recently the underground cities at Kaymaklı and Derinkuyu near Nevşehir have been opened up for tourists. These also were early Christian centers and must have housed several thousand people in the eighth and ninth centuries. They extend downward in the earth for at least eight floors in a maze of tunnels and rooms and were easily defended by blocking the entrance with large rocks. The sheer mechanics of organization, supply, and administration of such communities are staggering. A short, interesting description of life in such a place can be found in Xenephon's *Anabasis*. In relating the retreat of the Greek army of Ten Thousand from Babylon to the Black Sea he describes a village in which they were entertained briefly in the winter: "The houses here were underground, with a mouth like that of a well, but spacious below; and while entrances were tunnelled down for the beasts of burden, the human inhabitants descended by a ladder... It was here also that the village chief instructed them about wrapping small bags round the feet of their horses and beasts of burden when they were going through the snow; for without these bags the animals would sink in up to their bellies."*

TAVIUM — BÜYÜK NEFES KÖY

The site of Tavium has yet to be excavated. It is located near Büyük Nefes Köy which is about forty kilometers west of Yozat.** During the time when the area was inhabited and ruled by Galatians (from the third century B.C. onwards) it was one of the capitals of the three Celtic tribes, the Tectosages, the Tolistobogii, and the Trocmi. King Deiotarus, ruler of the Tolistobogii and the Trócmi, was a good friend of Cicero who was governor of Cilicia in 50 B.C. Deiotarus entertained Julius Caesar in his fortress northwest of Ankara in 47 B.C. and was then charged with trying to assassinate Caesar. Cicero came to his defense and he was acquitted.

* Xenephon, **Anabasis** IV, v. 25-27; 36
** Bittel, Kurt, **Kleinasiatische Studien,** p.6.

BIBLICAL SITES IN TURKEY

ANCYRA — ANKARA

The present capital of Turkey, Ankara, was founded by Phrygians in the eighth century B.C. Among the interesting places to see there is what is left of the Temple of Augustus. This was reconstructed from an earlier temple as thanks to Augustus for the city's semi-independence. On the walls of that temple is an inscription in both Latin and Greek recording the public acts of Caesar Augustus which included a census (Luke 2:1). Parts of copies of this have also been found in Antioch of Pisidia (Yalvaç) and Apollonia (Uluborlu). The temple was originally to a Phrygian god, Men; it became a church at the beginning of the sixth century and remained such until the city was conquered by the Turks. The Crusaders held the city for about 100 years from 1101 to 1227. By 1354 it was part of the Ottoman Empire.

The seventh century citadel above the city is one of the best surviving Byzantine forts. While it may have been built about 630 A.D., many much older columns, capitals, and inscriptions were used in it. The west, south, and east curtain walls are punctuated with many pentagonal towers. On the south wall (the least protected side) several crosses are visable. Perhaps the builders hoped that those would help in the defense of the fortress.

The Church of St.Mary of the Armenians used to stand north of the city and north of the Çubuk Su. It was a twelfth century building which replaced an ancient pagan temple. Legend said that Paul visited it. Members of the British community living in Ankara were buried there. The church had been destroyed before 1933.*

There are a few other remains from antiquity in the city such as the Roman baths and a column of Justinian dated 562 A.D. Before one reaches the citadel, on the road that leads to the citadel, one comes to the Museum of Anatolian Civilizations where many of the treasures from Çatal Höyük, Kültepe, Gordium, Toprakkale, Carchemish, and many other archeological sites are

* Barnett R.D., "The European Merchants in Ankara", in **Anatolian Studies,** vol. 24, 1974, p. 135.

displayed with excellent taste and imagination. A much more recent monument is the large mausoleum of Atatürk (Anıt Kabir) on an opposite hill.

PESSINUS — BALLIHİSAR

The ruins of the city of Pessinus are about fifteen kilometers south of the town of Sivrihisar and on the left bank of the Sangarius (Sakarya) River. What is left include a theater and the foundations of the famous temple to Cybele. Pieces of the marble wall of the canal for the stream are still in place. A small museum protects some of the tombstones found on the necropolis. The King of Pergamum, Attalus I, was associated with moving the sacred black stone supposed to represent the Mother of the Gods (Magna Mater Magnum Idaea) from that temple to Rome in 204 B.C. to help defend the city against Hannibal.

81

The case for Paul's having visited Pessinus is stronger than that for Kayseri, Tavium, or Ankara. The case is based on these facts: Pessinus was on the Persian Royal Road — the main highway east and west; Paul did travel through Phrygia and Galatia north of the province of Asia and a plausible route would have been along the Sakarya valley; and he did consider entering Bithynia on his second journey (Acts 16:6-8) so he could have been even farther north than Pessinus. One problem is in establishing what the boundaries of these provinces were at the time he was there and what they were in the writer's knowledge. As no other outside evidence has come to light yet to point one way or another for his route, the speculation remains.

ANTIOCH OF PISIDIA — YALVAÇ

About fifty-six kilometers west of Akşehir by winding mountain road is the Turkish town of Yalvaç, the place on the edge of the Antioch of Pisidia mentioned in the New Testament. The earliest written history of the city probably goes back to some time between 301 and 280 B.C. when Seleucus Nicator founded and named it, as he did many others, for his father. An earlier Phrygian settlement there was located around a temple. The population was a mixture of local Phrygians and colonized Jews, Romans, and Greeks who came from Magnesia on the Meander. While the original Anatolians spoke their own language, Greek was by Paul's time the language most likely to be understood by all. Latin was used for official governmental purposes and Hebrew probably was taught through the synagogue. The principal deity in Antioch was Cybele; Men, the main Anatolian male god, also was worshipped there.

82

The first mention of Pisidian Antioch in Acts (13:14) is when Paul on his first missionary journey arrived there from Perga and addressed the congregation in the synagogue on the Sabbath with his first recorded sermon. He told them of the forgiveness of sins that had come through Jesus. The inclusive form of Paul's salutation suggests that there were others than Jews in that first congregation: "Men of Israel and you who worship our God, listen to me" (Acts 13:16). What he said aroused the interest of those gathered so that they asked him to come back and speak again the next Saturday. It also must have been widely discussed since the next week "almost the whole city gathered to hear the word of God" (Acts 13:44). One can imagine the annoyance of the regular attenders of the synagogue at finding a crowd of what must have seemed to be curiosity seekers taking over their place of worship, and they reacted predictably and jealously against Paul. Paul and Barnabas rebuked the Jews for their lack of hospitality in much the same way Jesus had rebuked his followers when they had interfered with the children who wanted to be near him. That could not have endeared them to the congregation. The Gentiles rejoiced that they were to be included in the chance for salvation, but they were not influential enough. With the encouragement of the dissatisfied Jews, some important men and women managed to expel Paul and Barnabas from the city (Acts 13:50).

Paul may have visited Antioch again on his second and third missionary journeys, but only Derbe and Lystra are mentioned in Acts 16:1. Since he went from Lystra through the Phrygian and Galatian regions to Alexandria Troas he could well have also returned to Antioch. The account of the third missionary journey is even less specific, giving only the region names (Acts 18:23). He does talk in II Timothy 3:11 about the persecutions he suffered there which could refer to being expelled from town, and in Galatians 4:13 he refers to a "bodily illness" that first drove him to that country. But what the illness was (malaria? trachoma? jaundice?) or just where he went to recover is not specified.

However long he stayed in Antioch, his influence and that of Barnabas spread throughout the region and continued to bear fruit. But the angry Jews of Antioch and Iconium followed him to Lystra where they managed to incite the crowd against him.

Very little is left of Pisidian Antioch today. University of Michigan excavations begun before World War I were resumed briefly in 1924. Some of those findings are in the museum in Yalvaç. There is the propylaea of the acropolis with a number of carved stones, many with bulls' heads, the remains of a Byzantine church, and those of a basilica. Much of the building stone that once littered the ground has been carried off to be used again in other places. A short section of the Roman aqueduct is still standing in place north of the city.

ICONIUM — KONYA

The Bible does not say much about what happened to Paul and Barnabas in Iconium except that their work was effective enough that they antagonized the people there and had to flee. But in the apocryphal *Acts of Paul and Thecla* there is a legend which may have a grain of truth to it. In summary, the passage tells about Thecla's having heard Paul preach at Iconium and having embarrassed him in her determination to be baptised. There must have been a row because they were brought before the judge who condemned Paul to be whipped and expelled and Thecla to be burned. She was saved by a timely heavy rain and escaped to follow Paul to Antioch. She put on boys' clothes hoping to be allowed to stay with him in that disguise. That was unsuccessful, and she was next thrown to the wild beasts, but she managed to get away again and live to a ripe old age. Much of the story is implausible, but if it is at all true some of it might lead one to wonder if Paul's attitude toward women was influenced by her importunities. Along with Thecla's romantic adventures, however, there is a description of Paul that may reflect what he actually looked like: A man "of a low stature, bald on the head, crooked thighs, handsome legs, hollow-eyed; had a crooked nose; full of grace; for sometimes he appeared as a man, sometimes he had the countenance of an angel."* One wonders also if he was swarthy in complexion because of the Roman commandant in Jerusalem who confused him with an Egyptian who had instigated a riot (Acts 21:38).

84

As in Antioch, Paul and Barnabas used the synagogue in Iconium as their forum from which they could address those who would be interested in what they had to say. At each place they spoke first to the Jewish people and only when they had been rejected by them did they turn more of their attention to the Gentiles. In Iconium they caused a split among the people, both Gentiles and Jews being on each side. Those against them were more influential and got the support of the authorities, but Paul and Barnabas were warned in time enough to escape being stoned there.

Iconium is on the western edge of a great plain where clouds of dust in summer and blizzards of snow in winter sometimes sweep across the city. It is an extremely old city, its origins going at least to Hittite times in the third millennium B.C. Besides the Hittites, some of the people who have occupied it are Phrygians, Lydians, Persians, Byzantines, Mongols, Selçuks, and Ottomans. Seleucids, Pergamenes, and Crusaders also held it for various periods.

Directions for seeing the area are available at the Ministry of Tourism and Information Bureau near the Mevlana Museum in the center of the city.

Today the most interesting monuments in the city are the beautiful Selçuk mosques and schools and the monastery of the great poet Celâl-ed-din Rumî, mystic

---

* **The Apocryphal New Testament,** p. 100.

and head of the Whirling Dervishes (Mevlevî Dervişler). His mystic order has had a profound influence on Turkish Islam ever since the thirteenth century. An inscription on one of the walls of the tomb-museum in the monastery gives a typical saying of this Muslim Master: "Come in whoever you are, infidel, fire-worshipper, idolater. Ours is not a house of despair. Come in however often you may have broken your vows."

LYSTRA — GİLİSTRA?, ILİSTRA?

Lystra is identified by some with the village of Gilistra lying about thirty-five kilometers southwest of Konya and slightly north of Hatunsaray. Another possibility is the village of Ilistra just west of Karaman. It was in the southerly area of Roman Galatia called Lycaonia. Although Lystra had little commercial or strategic importance, Caesar Augustus located some veteran Roman soldiers in the city about 6 B.C. for protection against the tribes from the Taurus Mountains to the south. This action may shed light on Paul's comment that he had been beset with danger from robbers: soldiers were necessary there because the roads between the sea coast and central Anatolia were favorite haunts of bandits up until recent times.

A complicated incident is reported in Acts concerning the visit of Paul and Barnabas to Lystra. Paul noticed in the group gathered to listen to him a lame man whose bearing impressed him. Some extraordinary strength passed from Paul to the man who thereupon was cured. The miracle caused a commotion in the crowd, and people began shouting in their native language, Lycaonian, that the strangers had supernatural powers, that they were gods. The account here suggests that Paul understood and spoke that language in addition to Greek and Hebrew.* There was a temple to Zeus just outside the town; the priest was informed of the miracle and the people's interpretation of it, and so he at once prepared a welcome suitable for gods descended to earth. Barnabas was called Jupiter; was he the taller of the two? Paul was taken for Mercury because he was the spokesman. The

---

* Metzger, H., **Les Routes de Saint Paul dans l'Orient Grec.** p.17.

idea of being worshipped was of course blasphemy to Paul and Barnabas who acted promptly by denying the identification, stating their Christian beliefs, and tearing their clothes to avert any evil that might come of the presumption. But the crowd was excited and some of the Jews from Antioch and Iconium who had been waiting to do violence to Paul and Barnabas took this chance to turn the love to hatred. The crowd became a mob, stoning Paul. He was saved only by his friends forming a circle around him (Acts 14:8-20).

It is worth noting that Paul was never a coward. When he had a difference of opinion he held to his position although it meant that he and Barnabas parted company. Although he had been almost killed in Iconium and Lystra he returned to those places shortly afterwards.

When Paul was in Lystra on his second missionary journey (Acts 16:1-3) he met a young disciple named Timothy. Timothy's mother was Eunice, a Christian Jew, and his father was a Gentile. Timothy may have been part of the circle that protected Paul when he was stoned there earlier, but that cannot be proven. Timothy was well regarded by the church in Lystra and became a close friend of Paul's and, upon circumcision, his companion through most of that journey. He was also at Ephesus with Paul on his third journey, with him at Corinth (Acts 18:5), and a companion of his in prison, probably in Rome (Hebrews 13:23).

The history of Lystra, outside of its mention in the New Testament, appears to be undistinguished. There is a Hittite inscription about a King Larbanas that mentions a place called Lusna which may be Lystra, but that has not been established. What ruins there are at both Gilistra and Ilistra now have not been studied so almost nothing is known other than that the city was a Roman colony and that it conformed to the general history of the area.

DERBE — KERTİ HÖYÜK?, UNU HÖYÜK?, AŞIRAN HÖYÜK?, DEĞLE?

Paul and Barnabas went from Lystra to Derbe after Paul had recovered from being stoned.

CENTRAL TURKEY

An altar stone has been found in Kerti Höyük (see photo on p. 39) with an inscription that has the names of Derbe and Bishop Michael carved on it. Without other evidence of the city it is unfair to say it establishes the original site of Derbe because such stones are often moved. However it is probable that one of three tumuli near Karaman is the actual site. Değle (near Bin Bir Kilesi and Madenşehir) is a fourth possibility. The stone in question and another from Lystra are in the courtyard of the Konya Arkeoloji Müzesi. The present-day traveller who wishes to try to find Derbe would be well advised to engage a local guide in Karaman.

Derbe was the royal seat of the tyrant (absolute ruler) Antipater Derbetes who was also known as Antipater the Pirate. A hundred years before Paul and Barnabas were there, Antipater had entertained Cicero while he was governor of the neighboring province of Cilicia. Derbe was the last Roman city on the road to the east, so it was the point at which customs were collected.

No details of Paul's first stay in Derbe are reported, and the only other possible reference to it outside of its being mentioned in the second journey is the identification of one of Paul's companions between Greece and Troas as "Gaius the Doberian" or "Gaius the Derbaean." Paul and Barnabas both spoke to people in Derbe and won many converts (Acts 14:21); their ties with the people there continued strong enough that Paul returned a year or so later.

CHAPTER VII
THE GULF OF ATTALIA

SELECTED REFERENCES:

Attalia: Acts 14:25
Perga: Acts 13:13-14; 14:25
Myra: Acts 27:5-6
Patára: Acts 21:1-2

ATTALIA — ANTALYA

The area of Attalia (modern Antalya) is one of the most beautiful in all Turkey. It sits on sheer cliffs above the blue Mediterranean with a green plateau stretching behind the city to magnificent pine forests. To the west great mountains rise straight out of the sea.

The city was founded in the second century B.C. by Attalus II, the King of Pergamum, and was named for him. It replaced Side as the main port for the area. Side has always been exposed to all the storms on the Mediterranean; safe entrance to it was the occasion for great rejoicing both by those on board ship and those on land. Thus Attalia quickly became the commercial center of the Gulf as it had the better natural harbor.

Plutarch, in telling about Pompey's campaign against the Cilician pirates in the first century B.C., reports that the pirates observed certain secret rites including those of Mithra in Olympus just west of Attalia on the Gulf. This fire worship may well have been in connection with the natural fire known as the Chimera that has burned on a hillside there for centuries and is still visible at night from the sea.

Attalia is not named when Paul and Barnabas and Barnabas's cousin, John Mark, went from Paphos to Perga on their first journey (Acts 13:13), but either Side or

Attalia would have been possible ports. Or they may have sailed straight to the Perga wharf on the Cestrus (Aksu) River. On their way back from Iconium they came through Perga and sailed from Attalia to Antioch. No other mention is made of Attalia in the Bible, nor is there any comment about Paul's missionary work there.

Some evidences of early Christianity are still to be seen in Antalya. The archeological museum in the city formerly was in the ruins of the thirteenth century Selçuk mosque of Ala-ud-din Kaikubad I. (It now has moved to a new building.) In common with many other buildings around the Mediterranean the mosque was previously a Byzantine basilica built in the seventh century A.D. using second century B.C. materials. The museum houses some sarcophagi from Perga and a casket of bones reputed to be those of St. Nicholas (see the comments under Myra). Both the Great Mosque (Ulu Cami) and Kesik Minare Mosque were Byzantine basilicas also. The latter was the fifth century Church of the Panaghia and was decorated with finely carved marble.

PERGA — PERGE, MURTUNA

Perga was an old city even in the first century. Its name (which is not Greek) indicates that its origin dates from pre-Greek times. Alexander the Great passed through it twice while the Pergaeans offered no resistance to him although it was a walled city with a citadel. In Roman times the main streets were over twenty-one meters wide. They were lined with Ionic colonnades and a water channel ran down their center in a series of small waterfalls as in Antalya today. Behind the colonnades stood the shops. Of the early buildings the stadium and the theater have survived the ravages of earthquakes and wars with the least damage. In fact this stadium which could seat about fourteen thousand people is one of the best preserved in Turkey. The temple of the Pergaean Artemis according to a writer of the time was "a marvel of size, beauty, and workmanship." Its location has yet to be established; it may have been where there are now ruins of a Byzantine church on a hill to the southeast of the city.

THE GULF OF ATTALIA

Perga is on a rise not far from the Cestrus River which was navigable in Paul's time. It was not a seaport in terms of its being directly on the Mediterranean even then, but rather it was more easily defended where it was: its distance from the open sea made it less vulnerable to piracy.

Two people stand out among the early residents of Perga. Apollonius was a third century B.C. astronomer and mathematician who believed that the movements of heavenly bodies in the universe were explainable by orbits within orbits: that the moon went around the earth as the earth went around the sun. He was much ahead of his time in his theories of astronomy, so much so that the ideas had to be rediscovered during the Renaissance.

Plancia Magna was unusual for a second century A.D. woman: she held the highest city office during her life, that of *demiurgus* or magistrate. She must have been well-to-do for a number of inscriptions record her gifts to the city.

Paul and Barnabas went through Perga on their way to and from Antioch on their first journey (Acts 13:13, 14:25). John Mark was with them at first but left them at Perga to return to Jerusalem. The reason for that must have been such that Paul doubted his commitment to the cause. Later when Paul and Barnabas were about to start on their second journey from Antioch they had a sharp dispute over John Mark's worthiness. Paul refused to have him go along, so John and Barnabas went to Cyprus while Paul chose Silas to accompany him.

Paul talks in II Corinthians 12:7 and in Galatians 4:13-14 of bodily illness that brought him to Galatia the first time. It may have been on that account that he did not stay long in Perga the first time. Whatever the illness was, it seems to have improved in time in the dry mountain air to the north.

The second theory of why they did not stay long in Perga is that their interview with Sergius Paulus, the proconsul of Cyprus, had made them want to hurry to the Roman colony in Antioch of Pisidia. This interpretation may lay too much stress on the lasting importance of that meeting with a cultured Roman who could have been more interested in the pursuits of the mind than the salvation, in Christian terms, of his soul. It is interesting, however, that this is the point in Acts (13:9) that Luke begins to call Paul by his Roman name rather than his Jewish "Saul."

On their return from Antioch they did stay in Perga long enough to preach and talk with people there (Acts 14:25). Nothing else is told about the city or their time there.

MYRA — DEMRE

Myra is one of the ancient coastal cities of the Gulf of Antalya visited by Paul, Luke, and Aristarchus (Acts 27:5-6). It is where as prisoners they changed boats on their way to Rome in 60 or 61 A.D. In Myra the centurion Julius found a ship from Alexandria headed to Italy by way of Cnidus. They had hard sailing throughout the whole trip; Luke's account speaks of headwinds from Sidon to Myra, of slow headway to Cnidus, of wind continuing against them to Crete, and of the fierce northeastern Boreas that raged for days on end and finally shipwrecked them in Malta.

For foreigners the most interesting old building in Myra today is the Church of St. Nicholas built over the tomb of the saint who was martyred during the reign of Diocletian. The church is not much to look at. Its foundations go back to the fourth century when Nicholas was bishop of Myra. During the invasions of the Saracens in the eleventh century the saint's bones may have been moved to Bari in southern Italy where his fame increased. In fact, he is known as Nicholas of Bari in many parts of the world. He is the patron saint of the Russian, Greek, and Silician peoples, and also of children and sailors. (Myra was the seat of the god of pagan sailors also.)

The legend about St. Nicholas in Myra concerns a poor man who had three marriageable daughters but no way to provide their necessary dowries. St. Nicholas slipped under their window one night and tossed three purses of gold into the house to save them from prostitution. These purses have become the three gold balls identifying a pawnbroker's shop. This custom of giving gifts in secret was first observed on the eve of his day, December 6. This is still so in northern Europe. Later in the west the observance was moved to December 25 and his name corrupted to Santa Claus for English-speaking children.

In addition to the ruins of the church there is a Roman theater in Myra and an unusual rock necropolis.

93

PATARA — GELEMİŞ

The ruins of Patara consist of the large Hadrian granary, the city's triumphal arch, a theater with a long inscription, a sixth or seventh century Christian basilica, Lycian and Roman tombs, the baths, and a temple to Apollo. One of the chief centers of the worship of Apollo was here as was also the famous oracle of Apollo. Patara was the flourishing port for the city of Xanthus (Kınık) some ten kilometers up the Xanthus (Koca Çay) River. Xanthus was the ancient capital of the province of Lycia. While Xanthus was more heavily populated. Patara perhaps covered more acreage. Homer speaks of the area as the home of one of the heroes of the Trojan War. The port area has been erased by the shifting sands and the edge of the city is no longer immediately on the sea. In Paul's time it appears it was a good all-weather harbor.

As Paul and Luke returned from Miletus to Jerusalem at the end of the third journey they stopped in Patara. Here they probably changed from a small coastwise ship to a large one that could cope with the open Mediterranean (Acts 21:1-2).

CHAPTER VIII

TURKEY'S AEGEAN AND MARMARA AREAS

SELECTED REFERENCES:

Cnidus : Acts 27:7
Miletus : Acts 20:15-38; II Timothy 4:20
Trogillium : Acts 20:15
Colossae : Colossians
Hierapolis : Colossians 4:13
Adramyttium : Acts 27:2
Assos : Acts 20:13-14
Alexandria Troas : Acts 16:8-11; 20:5-12; II Corinthians 2:12-13;
    II Timothy 4:13

CNIDUS — KNİDOS

The first location of Cnidus was half-way along the Datça peninsula. The residents moved it to its present site both on the Island of Tropium and on the mainland in about 365 B.C. The island is now connected to the mainland by a low, narrow isthmus which forms two small good harbors. Its citizens grew wealthy from commerce; the peninsula was famous for its wine. It was a center of culture: two theaters and an odeum suggest that entertainment was important to these people. The city also had a good medical school. Praxiteles' most famous statue, that of the nude Aphrodite, was bought by the city after the people of Cos rejected it in favor of a more modest and less celebrated woman. The original of the Cnidus statue is still being hunted; the best copy is in the Vatican Museum.

Ctesias, the Persian historian, was a native of Cnidus as was Sostratus, the builder of the Pharos at Alexandria. The Pharos was a lighthouse considered one of the Seven Wonders of the ancient world. Eudoxus, one of the great astronomers, was also born in Cnidus. He perhaps was the head of Plato's Academy when Aristotle joined it in Plato's absence in 367 B.C. Eudoxus had his own school later in Cyzicus. He made a map of the stars and invented the horizontal sun dial.

There were a number of temples in the city, among them ones to Dionysus and Aphrodite. Games were celebrated there in honor of Apollo and Poseidon. The agora, the Temple of Aphrodite, the odeum, and two theaters can be seen in the ruins, thanks to recent excavations.

96

Cnidus was the last landfall mentioned in Asia Minor in Paul's journey from Jerusalem to Rome. He had been put on an Egyptian ship in Myra which sailed up the coast to Cnidus; because of headwinds they took a good many days to reach it (Acts 27:7). They probably did not anchor there because of the inclement weather which continued and in fact got much worse. Instead, they went on to Fair Havens in Crete where Paul advised them to winter, but, a southerly breeze springing up, the captain put out to sea again hoping for a better harbor. The wind changed and "for days on end there was no sign of either sun or stars, a great storm was raging, and our last hopes of coming through alive began to fade" (Acts 27:20).

They had run out of food before Paul saw a vision in which he was promised safe journey for himself and all on board. After two weeks they were shipwrecked, but all were saved: some swam to land, some paddled ashore on planks or parts of the broken ship. It was the island of Malta where they landed and then spent the winter. With better weather they continued on to Rome where according to tradition Paul immeasurably strengthened the church, wrote some of his undying letters, was tried as an incendiary in the great fire during the reign of Nero, and was executed.

MILETUS — BALAT

Miletus is an ancient city which seems to have been inhabited by settlers between the end of the Minoan (1600 B.C.) and the Mycenean (1200 B.C.) periods. It was an important port at the mouth of the Meander (Menderes) River, a natural outlet for Phrygian trade. That trade was carried on with Egypt and with the several colonies Miletus started on the Black Sea. Of those, Sinope and Cyzicus on the Marmara were founded before the mid-seventh century B.C.

Quite early the city was distinguished as the residence of philosophers and historians. Thales, who lived there from 640 to 546 B.C., is credited with being the founder of Greek geometry, astronomy, and philosophy. He predicted that an eclipse of the sun would occur in 585 B.C. It did — on the 28th of May. He propounded the theory that the "world stuff" retains its identity unchanging. While his "stuff" was water, that train of thought has led scientists to nuclear physics today. Anaximander was associated with Thales in Miletus. Only fragments of his work are left. They show that he believed that the universe was a totality and that its phenomena were subject to laws rather than to the whims of the gods. The famous hetarea Aspasia grew up there. Aspasia became the mistress of Pericles; her home in Athens was the salon for a famous group of writers and philosophers including Socrates.

Miletus was sacked by the Persians under Darius in 494 B.C. and he massacred its inhabitants. It was captured again by Alexander the Great in 334 B.C. But rather than being destroyed by carnage or looting, its end, like that of Ephesus, came because its harbor silted up and its commerce stopped. Lade which was once an island off the coast is now a hill far inland, and still the Meander River carries the soil of Anatolia farther and farther out into the Aegean. The bay of Miletus in early times separated it from Priene twenty kilometers to the north and extended east as far as Heracleia on the northeast shore of the Gulf of Heracleia, now Bafa Gölü.

Today one can climb around the impressive Greco-Roman theater and the Baths of Faustina. The main part of the city is on low ground which often is flooded and therefore hard to see clearly. The city's most important temple was located about twenty kilometers south in Didyma (Didim). It was the Temple of Apollo, the third largest structure in the Hellenic world, outdone only slightly by the Temple of Artemis in Ephesus and the temple in Samos. Associated with it was the oracle of Apollo which rivalled the oracle of Delphi in Greece in importance.

Paul's visit to Miletus came at the end of his third journey as he was hurrying to get to Jerusalem by Pentecost. He had chosen to put in at Miletus rather than at Ephesus because, although he wanted to see the elders of the congregation there, he did not want to spend a lot of time in Asia. One suspects Paul would have been faced with a complicated series of social and business engagements if he had stopped at Ephesus. However, although the riot at Ephesus was only a few months past also, there is no suggestion in Luke's account that Paul stayed away because of concern about hostility he might meet there.

The elders made the trip to Miletus and Paul spoke to them warning them to be alert in keeping watch over their flock and to work to support themselves and the weak because "happiness lies more in giving than in receiving" (Acts 20:35). He told them he was going to Jerusalem because of an inner compulsion, but he also predicted his approaching imprisonment. (That is, if one accepts the speech as being Paul's and not an ex post facto composition of Luke's.) "For myself, I set no store by life; I only want to finish the race, and complete the task which the Lord assigned to me, of bearing my testimony to the gospel of God's grace" (Acts 20:24). He reminded them he had been honest with them in giving them the full Christian message. Was he trying to say that this was not a mystery religion, the secrets of which were revealed only to a privileged few at the top of the priesthood? "I have kept back nothing; I have disclosed to you the whole purpose of God" (Acts 20:27).

The parting was an emotional one; the elders accompanied him to the ship feeling sorry for themselves that they would not see him again or have the encouragement and inspiration of his presence.

TROGILLIUM

Neither the New English Bible nor the Revised Standard Version includes the reference to Trogillium in Paul's journey from Assos to Miletus. It is, however, in the King James Version in Acts 20:15. Trogillium is on the cape where the Turkish mainland comes within a kilometer of Samos. The north slope of the mountain which forms the headland, Mt. Mycale (Samsun Dağı), was the place of the Panionian shrine. This was sacred to Poseidon, the god of the sea; one of his chief altars was located here. The Pan Ionic festival of the twelve cities of the Ionic League (Miletus, Myus, Priene, Samos, Ephesus, Colophon, Lebedus, Teos, Erythrea, Chios, Clazomenae, and Phocaea) was celebrated here. This Ionic confederation was more a sacred than a political union; the cities were autonomous although they did support and defend each other on occasion. It is quite possible that ships sailing from Chios and Samos to Miletus would regularly call at Trogillium for sailors to go ashore briefly and sacrifice to Poseidon although the festival by Paul's time had been overshadowed by another held in Erythrea.

COLOSSAE

Colossae has very few archeological remains uncovered and the place is not often visited. In the early 1930's one of the authors and Miss Olive Greene tried to find the site with the aid of the only guidebook to the area in existence then, a *Handbook for Travellers in Asia Minor* edited by Major-General Sir Charles Wilson in 1895. The guidebook said that Colossae was situated at "the head of the gorge, a little below the junction of three streams."It was an occasion like the discovery of a cave full of treasure when we finally made out the citadel with some of its walls still standing, a necropolis, and the cavea of a theater.

We are told by Herodotus that Colossae was an important city in his day. In Xerxes' march to Sardis and later to Thermopylae he stopped in Colossae in about 481 B.C. Another famous Persian, Cyrus the Younger, marched through in 401 B.C. Pliny the Elder, the first century A.D. naturalist, says that Colossae was one of several famous cities, perhaps because of the revenue from a soft wool dyed a purple "colossinus."

Apparently the city diminished in importance because of the rise of Laodicea and Hierapolis. It was destroyed in the great earthquake of 60 A.D., but people continued to live there into the eighth century A.D. Arab and Turkish invasions took their toll; now the closest town is Honaz on the slopes of Mt. Cadmus (Honaz Dağı) to the south.

Scholarship is divided over whether the Letter to the Colossians is genuinely Paul's or not; the weight seems to be in favor of his authorship. The main thesis of the letter is the need to keep the truth of the gospel pure, to guard it from the heresy of a syncretism of Judaism and pagan religions. Paul may here have been referring to the priests of the mystery cults, people who "try to enter into some vision of their own" (Colossians 2:18). Or he may have been talking about other oracular events. The first readers of the letter would have understood what Paul was referring to; he did not need to spell out for them or to immortalize the details of that heresy. Today we are left free to interpret his meaning for ourselves and for our time.

Paul probably did not visit Colossae; the Christian communities there and in the neighboring cities were the result of the work of Epaphras. Paul knew of them through Epaphras who was in prison with him in Caesarea or in Rome.

Another source of Paul's information about Colossae undoubtedly came from the slave, Onesimus, to whom he became deeply attached. Onesimus's owner was Philemon of Colossae, the one to whom the remarkable Letter to Philemon was addressed. Paul had apparently converted Onesimus to the Christian faith; he loved him as a son, and saw in him the possibility of a leader in the church. The letter pleads with Philemon to free Onesimus and return him to Paul. So far there is no proof that this happened, but it is remarkable if it is only coincidental that Ignatius, the Bishop of Antioch at the end of the first century, talks about an Onesimus who was Bishop of

Ephesus about the time that the group of Paul's letters was published, and that this "personal" letter was included.

HIERAPOLIS — PAMUKKALE

The presence of a hot spring at Hierapolis and the spectacular calcium deposits from its water spilling over the nearby hillside suggest that there should be evidence of an early settlement there. The oldest inscription found so far, however, indicates it was founded by Eumenes II, King of Pergamum, in the latter part of second century B.C.; it soon became a busy industrial center.

Pagan worship in the city centered around Cybele, Apollo, Artemis, Men, Poseidon, and Pluto. Underneath the Temple of Apollo has been found the Plutonium, an opening in the earth from which a deadly gas still comes. The temple is between the pool where the hot spring rises and the large theater on the side of the hill. To the north along the rim of the plateau is a long avenue of tombs.

Traditionally St. Philip is connected with the early church in Hierapolis. Fairly recently Italian archeologists have discovered his Martyrium, an octagonal chamber forming a double cross surrounded by a square. This is almost due north of the theater, also on the side of the hill. It was a fifth century A.D. building and did not last much more than 100 years. No tomb was found with it although that was expected. There are several ruins of churches, one not far from the baths, one on the main road leading to the necropolis.

Hierapolis is listed in the New Testament along with Laodicea as the center of Epaphras's work (Colossians 4:13). This was at the time Paul was writing to strengthen the message Epaphras was preaching and to condemn the "people who go in for self-mortification and angel-worship" (Colossians 2:18). Another less well-known resident of Hierapolis was Papias, a disciple of St. John and the author of the lost book called the *Sayings of Jesus.*

While Epapras was in that area, a young slave was growing up in Hierapolis, a boy whose original name is unknown but whom we call by the Greek for "Acquired," Epictetus. In his *Discourses* Epictetus often talks about the perfect missionary whose bed was the ground, whose only covering the earth and sky and a shabby cloak, and who must love those who misuse him in the service of God. One wonders what influence those early Christians, many of whom were slaves themselves, had on this Stoic philosopher.

ADRAMYTTIUM - EDREMİT

Adramyttium was founded in the fourth century B.C. by Lydian kings as one of their points of defense. Near the town rise the slopes of Kaz Dağı, the Mt. Ida, "many-fountained Ida" of Tennyson's "Oenone" where Paris gave up his pastoral life for a romance with Helen. Adramyttium is mentioned in the New Testament only as the home port of the ship which Paul and the centurion Julius and some other prisoners took from Caesarea of Phoenicia to Sidon and then to Myra (Acts 27:2).

ASSOS - BEHRAMKÖY

The beginnings of a city in Assos are before the first millennium B.C. An Ionian colony from Lesbos (Mytilene) settled there later, and then it came under Lydian and Persian domination. In 348 B.C., upon the death of Plato in Athens, Hermias, the tyrant of Atarneus, invited two of the members of the Academy to his court in Assos. They were Xenocrates and Aristotle. Aristotle married Pythias who was Hermias' adopted daughter; his own daughter was also called Pythias. It was in Assos that he started his first school where he taught for three years. Aristotle moved about 344 to Lesbos and then became the teacher of Philip of Macedon's young son, Alexander. Almost as soon as he moved to Pella he heard that Hermias had been captured by the Persians and tortured to death. That probably inspired his ode, *In Praise of Valor,* in memory of his friend.

Assos for a while was subject to the kings of Pergamum: it was known as Makhramion during

Byzantine times, but since the fourteenth century it has had little importance. Today its ruins are immediately next to the village of Behramköy.

At present one can see the city walls which are in good condition, the lookout towers, council chamber, theater, gymnasium, and the agora. A Byzantine church became a mosque in the fourteenth century; it is now unused. On the highest point of the volcanic hill of Assos there is the remains of the Doric temple of Athena that was built in the sixth century B.C. The view from it across the twelve kilometers of sea to Mytilene is spectacular. Although the Greek harbor several hundred meters below is no longer in use, the Roman one next to it still is for small fishing boats.

103

In Paul's third journey he went by land from Alexandria Troas to Assos, about a thirty-five kilometer trip; perhaps he walked, perhaps someone offered him a ride. Luke and the others with him took the ship and they met in Assos (Acts 20:13-14). From there they went across to Mytilene. Their next landfall was "opposite Chios (Sakız)" which probably was the Turkish coast, but no name has been given to the place. It might have been Erythrea (Ildır), one of the towns of the Ionian League which had a good harbor protected by off-shore islands and was a center for the worship of Poseidon then.

ALEXANDRIA TROAS — ODUN İSKELESİ

According to the historian Strabo, Troas was a renowned city. It was founded by Antigonus and Lysimachus at the command of Alexander the Great, and its fortifications date from that time. The city had a good but artificial harbor which helped it become a thriving commercial center. At the same time it was easily plundered so very little is left of what must once have been impressive. Among the thistles and trees that have grown up one can make out the city walls, theater, stadium, Herodes Atticus Bath and necropolis. The nearest village is Odun İskelesi about one kilometer to the north.

Paul visited Alexandria Troas at least twice; the first was when he and Timothy had wanted to go into Bithynia but had been prevented by the Holy Spirit. Instead they skirted Mysia and reached Troas where during the night Paul saw a vision of a Macedonian asking him to come help him (Acts 16:7-10). Probably Luke joined them here: from this point on in Acts the story is in the first person plural, "we." Rather than spending much time in Troas they found a ship quickly and sailed first to Samothrace and then went on to Neapolis (Kavala) and Philippi.

There is some doubt whether Paul went back through Troas again before he spent a week there on his way to Jerusalem and imprisonment; it is hard to follow Paul's movements with certainty from what is reported in Acts. Of course that is not Luke's fault: his purpose in writing is to show how Paul spread the Christian message, not where he spent the night. Luke, however, does give many more details about their sea voyages than their travels overland; perhaps he shows the eager curiosity of an amateur sailor.

In Troas the second time Paul spoke to the group that had gathered for the breaking of bread on Saturday night. The meeting went on until late, Paul himself speaking until midnight. Probably the room got stuffy from all the people gathered there and from all the lights burning. Finally a boy named Eutychus who was sitting on one of the window ledges went to sleep and fell three stories to the ground. He was picked up for dead, but Paul, who went down, looked at him and said, "Stop this commotion; there is still life in him" (Acts 20:10). After this incident Paul went back upstairs, had something to eat, and continued talking until sunrise. One supposes the room had gotten aired out a bit in the meantime.

It could be that during this visit to Troas Paul left his cloak behind in the excitement. Maybe it was used to cover Eutychus and keep him warm after his fall. Whatever the reason, Paul asks Timothy to "bring the cloak I left with Carpus at Troas, and the books, above all my notebooks" (II Timothy 4:13).

Troas is also mentioned in II Corinthians 2:12 when Paul comments that he was disappointed at not finding Titus there, and so he went on to Macedonia. This

Paulustor oder Tor der Kleopatra

Eski Camı
(Kilise Camii)

Alexandria Troas

Selçuk

Ephesus

Artemis

108

Ephesus

Meryemana

Smyrna

Pergamon

Sardes

110

Thyatira

Sardes

Philadelphia

Laodizea

Hierapolis

probably refers to his first visit to Troas when he did not
stay but quickly took the ship and went to Philippi.

*

* *

In describing the various sites of Anatolia, it is difficult
to stay strictly within the limits of only those mentioned in
the Bible. Some sites are there obviously only
incidentally; some others can be guessed at although they
are not named; and some perhaps were so well known
that mentioning them may have seemed unnecessary.
Archeology today has brought many places to our
attention which, although they do not appear on the
pages of the Bible, have added greatly to our knowledge
of people living in the Near East: Çatal Höyük,
Aphrodisias, and Troy to mention only a few. However,
two other places, Nicaea (İznik) and Byzantium or
Constantinople (İstanbul), have been so important in
subsequent Christian history that we are including a few
brief comments on them.

113

NICAEA — İZNİK

At the time of Paul's travels, Nicaea shared with
Nicomedia (İzmit) the rivalry for the most important city of
Bithynia. In 74 A.D. it was incorporated into the Roman
province of Asia and, in spite of being levelled in the
earthquake of 123 A.D., it continued to flourish.

The importance of Nicaea in Christian history is in the
two church meetings held there, the First Ecumenical
Council of 325 and the Seventh Ecumenical Council of
787. The outcome of the First Council of Nicaea was
primarily a condemnation of the teachings of Bishop
Arius. It also was the first attempt to establish the criteria
of Christian orthodoxy and membership by a creed. And it
admitted the principle of state-church cooperation.
Constantine delivered the opening address to the synod
which was convened in the imperial palace on about May
20th; he ended it with a brilliant banquet there on July
25th.

The Seventh Ecumenical Council was prompted by
the iconoclastic controversy. It was held in the Church of

St. Sophia, the ruins of which can be seen at the main crossroads in the center of the city. Among other things this council declared that icons deserved reverence (Gr. *proskynesis*) but not adoration (Gr. *latreia*) which was due to God alone. This statement was confirmed by Pope Adrian I, but partly because of an incompetent translation it was not acceptable generally in the West. For instance, the two words, *proskynesis* and *latreia*, were equated in the translation so it appeared that the Council ordered Christians to worship icons the same way they worshipped God. With this Council the division between Rome and Constantinople (which had been stimulated by the Fourth Ecumenical Council in Chalcedon in 451) became complete, the Roman Catholic Church and the Eastern Orthodox Church each going its own way.

BYZANTIUM, CONSTANTINOPLE — İSTANBUL

Semistra seems to be the name of the first settlement of people on the Golden Horn some time during the first millennium B.C. This was at the head of the Horn where the two streams, Cydaris (Ali Bey Suyu) and Barbysus (Kâğıthane Suyu), come together. In the ninth century B.C. the town of Lygus began on the headland of the cape now known as the Seraglio Point. Byzantium, according to legend, was founded by Byzas who followed instructions from the Oracle of Delphi for him to build "opposite those who were blind." That seemed strange until Byzas decided that the people of Chalcedon (Kadıköy) were blind for having occupied that bay rather than the more favorable point on the European side of the Bosphorus.

Byzantium was an important center of trade, and about 279 B.C. began to exact a toll from all who used the Bosphorus. Many different armies attacked it, those of Darius, Philip of Macedon, and Septimius Severus among them. It is not mentioned in the New Testament although the First Letter of Peter is addressed "to those of God's scattered people who lodge for a while in Pontus, Galatia Cappadocia, Asia, and Bithynia" (I Peter 1:1-2) — a quite general scattering it must be admitted. Beyond this there is an early Byzantine tradition which names St. Andrew, brother of Simon Peter and one of the twelve apostles, as the "first called" to this area and associates him with the claim that the See of Byzantium was apostolic in origin.

Byzantium became the capital of the Roman Empire under Constantine in 330 A.D. when he formally took up residence in the city. He had recognized Christianity in 313; it remained for Theodosius I in 391 and 393 to establish the new religion firmly as that of the state by forbidding the observance of all pagan rites, both in public and in private. He called the Second Ecumenical Council to meet in the Church of St.Irene in 381.

New Rome as it was first known, or Constantinople, continued as the capital of the Byzantine Empire until its conquest in 1453 by the Ottoman army under Sultan Mehmet II.

The most famous church of Eastern Christianity was built in Constantinople by the Emperor Justinian between 532 and 537. Awed by this triumph, he is quoted as exulting when the church was dedicated: "Glory be to God, who hath deemed me worthy to accomplish such a work! Oh, Solomon, I have surpassed thee!" Solomon's temple is only a memory, but St. Sophia continues to awe architect, church historian, and casual tourist alike.

In the Museums of Antiquities (Arkeoloji Müzeleri) near St. Sophia, in addition to the sarcophagus associated with Alexander the Great because of its friezes illustrating his battles, there are three smaller pieces of some interest and importance to biblical scholars. One is a small, irregular stone with what appears to be a child's lesson about seasons cut into it. This "Gezer calendar" has been dated tenth century B.C. and is the oldest extant bit of Hebrew writing. The second is the stone from the temple in Jerusalem which defined the boundary of the Holy of Holies, the point beyond which a Gentile was to enter only on pain of death. The inscription is in Greek so that there could be no plea of misunderstanding by one who trespassed. The third stone is known as the Siloam inscription. This is the inscription in Hebrew from the Hezekiah tunnel between the Pool of Siloam and the Spring Gihon in Jerusalem (II Chr. 32:30).*

In another of the buildings in this compound there is a fragment of the original treaty between the Egyptians and the Hittites that was made after the Battle of Qadesh about 1285 B.C.

İstanbul is rich with a thousand other details of our history, but the description of them lies outside the province of this book.

* See Josephus, **Wars of the Jews,** Bk. V, ch. 5:2. Also **The Interpreter's Dictionary of the Bible** for translations of the Gezer calendar (vol. I, p. 485) and the Siloam inscription (vol.4, p. 354).

CHAPTER IX

THE SEVEN CHURCHES OF REVELATION

SELECTED REFERENCES:

Ephesus: Revelation 1:11; 2:1-7; Acts 18:19-28; 19:1-41;
  Ephesians
Smyrna: Revelation 2:8-11
Pergamum: Revelation 2:12-17
Thyatira: Revelation 2:18-29; Acts 16:14
Sardis: Revelation 3:1-6
Philadelphia: Revelation 3:7-13
Laodicea: Revelation 3:14-22; Colossians 2:1; 4:13-16

The Seven Churches mentioned in The Revelation of John have long held a unique place among the sites to be visited in Asia Minor. It is generally thought that these seven were more a symbolic idea than a limited number needing immediate encouragement and admonition. But the impress of the apocalyptic message has given these particular churches qualities of both obscurity and importance which theologians are still struggling to interpret.

The places are well-known; all are close to İzmir and can be reached easily by public or private transportation. It is possible that the cities are named in the order of a regular circuit made by a messenger for the churches. Each is within a two- or three-day trip of the one before by horseback, given good travelling conditions; the longest stretch is the last leg between Laodicea and Ephesus. The seven could be visited in the order they are addressed without much retracing of one's steps.

Three are still living cities: Smyrna (İzmir), Philadelphia (Alaşehir), and Thyatira (Akhisar). Bergama is just to the side of Pergamum, Goncalı is below the hills of Laodicea, and the village of Sartmustafa is close to

Sardis. Three, Ephesus, Thyatira, and Laodicea, are mentioned elsewhere in the New Testament. Of the seven, Ephesus gives the visitor today the fullest sense of a complex, bustling metropolis at the turn of the Christian era . All have been studied by archeologists, but today active excavations are not being carried on in present-day Smyrna or Philadelphia. The work in the others varies according to funds and scholars available, possibility of important finds, complications with buildings currently in use on the sites, and many similar problems. Philadelphia and Thyatira show little of their Roman backgrounds; most of the buildings stones that may have made churches or theaters have been used so often for other purposes in the places that have been inhabited recently that their original identifying character has worn off or been defaced.

In the Roman Empire at certain periods of the first century all citizens were required to worship past and present emperors and also Roma, the female personification of Rome. Since most of the earliest Christians had been Jews and since Jews were exempt from bowing to Roman gods, these first Christians were also exempt. But as Christianity spread among the Gentiles, most Christians by the end of that century were not Jews. The religion of Jesus by then had become separate from Judaism. As pressure on the followers of Jesus to worship the Roman gods increased, more and more Christians were unable to bear the persecution and so fell away from their faith. Because of this the best evidence for the date of the writing of Revelation points to the last year or two of the reign of Domitian (81-96 A.D.) when persecution both in Rome and in the eastern provinces was frequent.

The author of Revelation, John, seems to have written expecting his work to be read aloud, not only in the seven churches he addressed but also throughout the area. He intended to be understood by the congregations as he also seems to have understood details in each of their backgrounds: the gleaming sun god of Thyatira, the famous ointment of Laodicea. His purpose was to prevent the disintegration of Christianity by clarifying and sharpening the alternatives facing Christians then: the

118

choices of worshipping Caesar or God. It is possible that he intentionally used the apocalyptic form of literature because he believed that that would be the most persuasive for his audience. He promised that, although the powers of evil are now in control of human affairs, God will intervene and overcome them to the glory of His name and the salvation of the faithful. John wished to make Christian martydom surpassingly attractive and the eternal punishment of paganism or apostacism irrefutable. For many people then, and even today, he succeeded.

119

EPHESUS — EFES

Ephesus is probably the most impressive archeological site in Turkey. It must have been colonized by the Greeks not later than the tenth century B.C. although Lydians and Carians occupied the site earlier. The Greeks brought their own goddess, Artemis, with them to Ephesus. (The statues of her in the museums in Selçuk and İzmir are not from Paul's time but are second century A.D. representations.*) For over a thousand years this goddess with her temple provided a focal point for the rich religious, economic, and cultural life of her worshippers.

Now hardly one stone can be seen of one of the most famous buildings in the world, the Temple of Artemis in Ephesus. Built on marshy ground not far from the Cayster (Küçük Menderes) River, it arose on a site occupied from time to time by several temples of which at least one dates from pre-Greek days. It faced west, toward the sea and the setting sun. Pliny the Younger tells us that the columns in front of the temple were carved with notable events in the life of the Greeks and that the statue of Artemis stood in the inner sanctuary. Some of the statuary from this temple is displayed in the New Hofburg Museum in Vienna. This temple was the first in the world to be constructed entirely of marble.

Ephesus must have been a beautiful city in its time. The usual approach was from the west, from the sea. A visitor, arriving on a trireme loaded with cargo, slaves, and

* H. Metzger, Conference, 6 April 1977

pilgrims bringing gifts to Artemis, must have been overwhelmed by the first view of her temple. As pilgrims approached from the west and looked to the right of the temple they would have seen the great theater on the slopes of Mt. Pion (Panayır Dağı) standing out in the brilliant Aegean sun. Even today, as the theater is being partially restored, one can almost hear the toga-clad audience cheering some hero on the stage or perhaps screaming against Paul. To the north of the theater one can see a decorated arch, the entrance to the stadium. A wide marble-paved arcaded street called the Arcadian Way stretched from the base of the theater several hundred meters to the harbor. It was lined with statues, porticos, and public buildings, one of which may have been the lecture hall of Tyrannus where Paul held daily discussions (Acts 19:9). Just north of the Arcadian Way is the church of the Virgin Mary or the Double Church where the Third Ecumenical Council was held in 431.

120

Another marble street stretches from the theater south to the library of Celsus where thousands of parchments and papyri were stored, protected from dampness and worms by a double wall, but not from earthquake or war. To the west of the library along the edge of the Hellenistic agora are stairs, the tumbled columns (each weighing eighty tons), and the exquisite decorations of the temple of Serapis, a composite Egyptian deity. Great drums of the eight marble columns supporting the architrave, each nearly a meter and a half in diameter, their capitals and entablature carved with the intricate acanthus leaves and universal egg and dart patterns, lie in front of the temple.

Returning to the library from the temple one continues up the long paved street toward the east, past the recently uncovered Temple of Hadrian, and on to the odeum, the little theater that is thought to have been covered with a roof because there is no provision for the rain water to be carried away. It held about 2,200 spectators. Here musicians played their flutes, lyres, and citharas, and poets recited from Homer and Hesiod.

Not far in front of the odeum is the foundation of what is thought to have been a temple that was later made into a church. A bull's head carved in the doorjamb once led

THE SEVEN CHURCHES

people to believe this was the tomb of St. Luke since the
bull's head was an ancient symbol for him.

When Paul was returning from Corinth to Ephesus he
brought Priscilla and Aquila with him. Here he stayed
briefly, talked in the synagogue where he was asked to
stay longer, and promised, "I shall come back to you if it is
God's will" (Acts 18:18-20). And so he left Ephesus for
Caesarea of Phoenicia and Jerusalem, completing that
second journey.

121

On his third journey he found several others engaged
in evangelism in Ephesus. Two of them were his earlier
friends, Priscilla (often called Prisca) and Aquila. We are
told in Acts 18:2-4 that Aquila was a Jew born in the
province of Pontus. Priscilla and Aquila had emigrated to
Rome, but with all other Jews they were forced to leave
the city under an edict of the Emperor Claudius and they
settled in Corinth where Paul met them when he visited
that city. Aquila's trade was that of a tentmaker. Since this
was also Paul's trade they became acquainted and Paul
lived with them in Corinth (Acts 18:3). They no doubt had
met each other in the synagogue.

Paul was able to continue speaking in the synagogue
in Ephesus for three months before he withdrew his
disciples and went to the lecture hall of Tyrannus.
According to one reading, Paul taught from the fifth to the
tenth hour, that is, from eleven to four, during the hottest
hours of the day when the hall was empty. This he did
every day for two years.

The troubles that Paul encountered in Ephesus are
scantily told by Luke, but the riot in Ephesus is one vivid
example of how people with business interests can join
with those who have strong religious beliefs to try to
prevent change. The sale of silver images of the temple
and of Artemis declined when Paul preached that "gods
made by human hands are not gods at all" (Acts 19:26). So
Demetrius, a leader of the silversmiths, told a group of
tradesmen that not only would a lot of people be out of
work, but "the sanctuary of the great goddess Diana will
cease to command respect; and then it will not be long

before she who is worshipped by all Asia and the civilized world is brought down from her divine preeminence " (Acts 19:27).

Demetrius was right in his judgment of the situation, and perhaps he can be considered to have won this skirmish. His speech caused an uproar in the city and the mob rushed into the large theater shouting, "Great is Diana of the Ephesians" for about two hours. The city clerk was called in to tell the crowd that it had legal recourse through the court for redress of injuries if the missionaries had done anything wrong, but that the rioters were in danger of prosecution if they continued. By then most of the people in the theater did not know why they had come in the first place. So the clerk dismissed the meeting and the city calmed down. However it was apparent to Paul that he had better leave. Calling the believers together, he said goodbye to them with words of encouragement and set off for Macedonia (Acts 19:28-20:1).

122

The entire sixteenth chapter of Romans, which is a series of personal greetings, is probably a note to a Christian congregation in Ephesus that somehow became attached to that book. The third verse of this series is a greeting to Prisca and Aquila who "risked their necks to save my life" (Romans 16:3). In I Corinthians 15:32 Paul writes, "If, as the saying is, I 'fought wild beasts' at Ephesus, what have I gained by it?" The beasts may have been human or they may have been lions from which, perhaps with the aid of Prisca and Aquila, he mercifully escaped.

Paul's second letter to the Corinthians from Ephesus (probably written in the same year as the first) reinforces a sense of frustration that one does not find in Acts: " ...We should like you to know, dear friends, how serious was the trouble that came upon us in the province of Asia. The burden of it was far too heavy for us to bear, so heavy that we even despaired of life" (II Corinthians 1:8).

How much of the suffering and persecution mentioned in other portions of II Corinthians (6:4-10, 11:23-27) occurred in Ephesus we do not know. In Romans 16:7 there is a word of greeting to "Andronicus and Junias my fellow-countrymen and comrades in captivity." This strenghthens the evidence that Paul was imprisoned in Ephesus.

Many scholars now believe that it was during an Ephesian imprisonment that Paul wrote Philippians, and perhaps also other letters now in the New Testament. A mute reminder of Paul's possible imprisonment there is a solid stone building sitting on a hill about one kilometer west of the theater and known today as St. Paul's Prison.

123

The actual facts of early Christian presence in the area, wrapped as they are in layers of the past, are difficult to discover. One tradition tells us that some years after the death of Jesus, perhaps about 40 A.D., the Apostle John came to Ephesus to live. The Church Fathers testify that he presided over the churches of Asia in the later years of his life,that he died a natural death, and was buried where the Church of St. John now stands in Selçuk. The early name of that place was Ayio Theológo which was transformed in common parlance through Ayo-thológo and Ayosoluk to a word meaningful to its present Turkish residents, Selçuk.* This name is in keeping with the Byzantine tradition of calling a town according to its most important church. Here it was the church of St. John Theologus, but that name in itself does not prove that he lived there. Ayasoluk was the name by which the town was known well into the present century. An early memorial connected with John's supposed grave was later enclosed in a small church. Under the Byzantine Emperor Justinian, the church became a cathedral. Some of its fallen columns have been set up again recently. Besides the nave there is a baptistery and a small chapel with some frescoes.

Another tradition, especially among Catholics, is that John brought Mary, the mother of Jesus, to Ephesus and that she lived out her days on a hilltop south of the city. Tradition is in itself sufficient evidence for a person who finds religious comfort in believing that she actually came here to live. But there is no direct evidence in the Bible. The assumption is that the disciple John was the disciple whom Jesus loved, and that he was also the author of the

* See Ramsay, **The Historical Geography of Asia Minor,** p. 110.

Gospel According to John which is traditionally associated with Ephesus.

The conflicting tradition is that John was martyred in 44. A.D. and that Mary died on Mount Zion in Jerusalem where the Church of the Dormition now stands.

The home of Mary, Meryem Ana, is now visited by over a hundred thousand pilgrims each year, of whom many are Muslims who revere her. The pilgrims come to drink the waters of the sacred spring, to meditate, to pray for health, and to breathe the atmosphere of what undoubtedly is an ancient spot of worship. In 1967 Pope Paul VI celebrated mass here, and prayed both in the Church of St. John and in the Double Church (the Church of St. Mary) in Ephesus itself. Pope John Paul II was here in November 1979.

In Revelation John claimed that he had a vision in which "one like a son of man" who is the first and last and living one commanded him to write "to the angel of the church at Ephesus." (Revelation 1:13-19, 2:1). To that church the words came from "the One who holds the seven stars in his right hand and walks among the seven lamps of gold" (Revelation 2:1). The burden of the letter was that the Ephesians had cooled in their faith: "you have lost your early love" (Revelation 2:4). These words were a reminder of the days of Paul a generation before when the first converts to faith in Christ were intense in their belief. "Fortitude you have," he said. But "think from what a height you have fallen; repent, and do as you once did." (Revelation 2:3, 5). He commended them for not compromising their beliefs as the Nicolatians did. For those who are faithful, John held out this promise: "To him who is victorious I will give the right to eat from the tree of life that stands in the Garden of God. " (Revelation 2:7). This promise John made in the name of the Spirit of his vision and of Christ.

SMYRNA — İZMİR

The area of Old Smyrna near Bayraklı across the bay from the present İzmir was inhabited during the first half of the third millennium B.C. Strabo says that the settlers were Leleges, but for that period of time he is not a reliable historian. Hittite remains in the area show that they were there at an early date. Apparently the Aeolian Greeks occupied the site of Old Smyrna around 1100 B.C. coming from islands in the Aegean. Before the Aeolians arrived, legends are our only source of information about Smyrna. Strabo, reporting one of these, tells us that the cities of both Smyrna and Ephesus were founded by the Amazons. One derivative gives "Smyrna" as the name of a certain Amazon. It would be outrageous to suggest that the Amazons of legend were the Hittites of history wearing kilts!

Herodotus reports how the Ionian Greeks, the people who built up a great civilization in central western Turkey, came to the shores of Anatolia. He says that certain Ionians, perhaps driven out of Greece by Dorian invaders from the north, had settled in Colophon, an ancient city some thirty-five kilometers south of Smyrna. It was famous for its squadrons of dogs used in battle and for its cavalry. However, the Colophonians expelled the refugee Ionians who thereupon fled to the Aeolian city of Smyrna. Then, while the Aeolians were attending a festival, the Ionians took over the city. This change from one branch of Greeks to another took place about 800 B.C. and is attested by shards found during recent excavations. According to legend, around that time the blind epic poet, Homer, was born and lived in this area.

About 600 B.C. Alyattes, the father of Croesus of Sardis, conquered and destroyed Smyrna. For nearly three hundred years, all through the classical Greek period, Smyrna remained a mere village or group of several small villages. Then it was awakened to glory and prosperity by Alexander the Great. The story goes that Alexander, soon after he came to the throne of Macedonia, defeated the Persians at Granicus about forty-five kilometers south of the Dardanelles. Pausing in Smyrna on his way to fresh victories at Sardis, Miletus, and Halicarnassus (Bodrum), he was out hunting on Mt. Pagus (Kadifekalesi) and slept near the sanctuary of the goddess Nemesis. She appeared to him in a dream and told him to move the people of Smyrna across the bay to the land below the hill which would make an excellent fortified citadel. The people checked with the local oracle, that of Apollo at Claros, and the answer came back,

> "Three and four times happy shall those men be hereafter/ Who shall dwell on Pagus beyond the sacred Meles."

This was unusually clear advice from an oracle, so the people moved without hesitation and the village that had its right shoulder to the bay became a city facing front on and electing its own magistrates both as part of the Kingdom of Pergamum and as part of the Roman province of Asia.

Being one of the oldest continuously inhabited communities of the world, İzmir has had many disasters: devastating earthquakes in 178 A.D. after which Marcus Aurelius ordered the city rebuilt, and again in 1688 and 1778; complete or partial destruction by Lydians, Arabs, Byzantines, Genoese, Turks, Crusaders, Tamerlane, Venetians, and Greeks. In spite of all this and more, İzmir has flourished continuously from Hellenistic times to the present.

Unfortunately there are few remains of the Hellenistic city. Mt. Pagus is there with its 160 meters of height, but what is left of its encircling crown of walls is the work of the Byzantine inhabitants. In the old stadium on the west side of Mt. Pagus we could discern seats in 1940, but now it is thickly covered with houses although its bowl shape remains. The ancient agora or marketplace, once surrounded by colonnades, still contains a row of columns set over a substructure of interesting architectural design.

Polycarp was an early member of the Christian church in Smyrna. He was bishop there from 115 to 156 A.D. Several contemporary accounts of him have been preserved along with some of his writing. There is a letter of his to the Philippians in which he says, "....the love of money is the root of all evil. Knowing therefore that as we brought nothing into this world, so neither may we carry anything out; let us arm ourselves with the armor of righteousness."*

Ignatius, the Bishop of Antioch, wrote to Polycarp, "Having known that thy mind towards God, is fixed as it were upon an immoveable rock; I exceedingly give thanks, that I have been thought worthy to behold thy blessed face, in which I may always rejoice in God... The times demand thee, as the pilots the winds; and he that is tossed in a tempest, the haven where he would be; that thou mayest attain unto God."**

127

The times were tempestuous ones for Polycarp. Towards the end of his life he went to Rome to talk with Bishop Anicetus about the controversy over the date of Easter. The meeting did not produce more than a harmonious agreement to differ, and Polycarp returned to Smyrna. Shortly thereafter in 156, persecution of the Christians began in Smyrna. During a festival and games there at which the proconsul, Statius Quadratus presided, eleven Christians, mostly from Philadelphia, were brought to be put to death in the stadium. Polycarp went into hiding on a farm on the outskirts of the city but he was betrayed, arrested, and brought back on the demands of the crowd. Statius Quadratus tried to make him deny his Christian faith, but he refused saying, "Eighty and six years I have served Him and He has done me no ill; how then can I blaspheme my King who hath served me?" The crowd shouted for him to be thrown to the lions, but the proconsul told them that the games were over. They angrily refused to release Polycarp or postpone his death and were satisfied only after they had succeeded in burning him at the stake.

Besides his example of martydom, Polycarp was important to the early church as a preserver of the purity of the Gospel. He was not a creative or deep thinker, but he was an accurate transmitter of the first traditions of Christianity. The shouts of the enraged crowd, as reported by Eusebius, are perhaps the highest tribute to him: "This is the teacher of Asia; this is the destroyer of our gods; this is the father of the Christians."

*The Apocryphal New Testament, "Epistle of Polycarp to the Philippians" p. 190.
* * Op. cit. "Epistle of Ignatius to Polycarp" pp. 186-187.

The letter to Smyrna in Revelation was probably written about sixty years before Polycarp's martyrdom. "These are the words of the First and the Last, who was dead and came to life again" (Revelation 2:8). In each of the letters the One speaking is characterized by some otherworldly quality. Poverty, slanders, and suffering were the common fate of most early congregations. The group in Smyrna was no exception to this (Revelation 2:9), but John told them not be afraid of suffering for he promised that it would not last long: "Only be faithful till death, and I will give you the crown of life... He who is victorious cannot be harmed by the second death" (Revelation 2:10-11).

PERGAMUM — BERGAMA

The origin of Pergamum is unknown, but such an easily defended hill would have been inhabited at a very early date. The main weakness of its defense was a lack of water. We ourselves can begin to sympathize with the plight of besieged soldiers as we walk around the hill on a summer day. We can also understand the reason for the inscription above many of the springs and fountains in Turkey: "From water comes all life."

Pergamum was first mentioned in Xenephon's *Anabasis* as the meeting place in 399 B.C. of Xenephon and the commander of the Spartans who had just defeated the Athenians in one of the Peloponnesian Wars. Nothing more is heard of Pergamum until after the death of Alexander the Great in 323 B.C. Then Lysimachus, one of his generals, took control of western Asia Minor. Later there was a series of kings named alternately Eumenes and Attalus who extended and strengthened their kingdom and spent some of their booty decorating the towering citadel of Pergamum with beautiful white marble structures. What is left of their contributions continues to attract people even now to their city.

In 133 B.C. Attalus III bequeathed the kingdom of Pergamum to the Roman government and it became known as the Province of Asia. The city of Pergamum remained one of the capitals for two and a half centuries, and was still a principal city of the province when the Book of Revelation was written.

One of the great events in the reign of the Attalid kings (263-133 B.C.) was the defeat of the Gauls in 230 B.C. The Gauls (related to those who settled in France) were invited by the king of Bithynia in 279 B.C. to come to Asia Minor as mercenaries in his private wars. After serving the king they settled in the area around Ankara, but they did not give up their warlike activities among their neighbors. They were so bloodthirsty that native soldiers were afraid to fight them, so instead many cities paid tribute to them.

However, King Attalus I of Pergamum determined to rid Asia Minor of these barbarians. Before his attack he prepared a sacrifice to the gods in order that the oracle might speak a word of encouragement to his frightened soldiers. The priest of the oracle announced the miracle that "Victory for the King" had appeared on the liver of the sacrificial animal. Attalus chose not to reveal to his inspired soldiers that he had written the words backwards on his hand and while helping examine the victim he had pressed his hand on the liver! Although outnumbered, the Pergamenes were victorious with no little thanks to their king's knowledge of human nature. This battle is commemorated in the famous statue of the Dying Gaul which is now in the Vatican Museum.

The large theater built into the hillside and extending upwards for seventy-eight rows of seats is impressive for its steepness. The site is fortunate in having almost perfect acoustics: actors in the orchestra can talk quietly and still be heard in the top rows. North of the theater is the Temple of Athena and between them are the few rough stones that are left of the famous library. To the south is the agora and the Altar of Zeus. Much of the marble of that is in the museum in Berlin. A number of other temples can be seen as can the large gymnasium, various parts of the city wall, and the aqueduct which brought water from springs in the distant hills to the cistern on the citadel.

The lower part of Pergamum is today known as Bergama. Its largest building of the Roman period is the Red Court (Kızıl Avlu), sometimes called the Red Basilica. It was probably built in the second century. A.D. and has a central hall three stories high with red brick walls some two meters thick. The Selinus (Bergama Çayı) River flows diagonally under the court. There is no question that the building was originally a center of worship, but just which god or gods were worshipped there is uncertain. It may first have been a temple to several Egyptian gods, among them Serapis. Later a raised floor was put in and it was used as a church dedicated to St. John the Apostle.

130

A museum where both archeological and ethnological items are well displayed is located on the main street of the city.

Also below the citadel and southwest of the city is the Asclepieum, the medical center of Pergamum.There are incubation rooms where patients lay on skins or on the ground and hoped, by being close to the gods of the earth and the underworld, that they would wake up healed. In addition there are the theater, the library, the temple to Asclepius, and, under the central square, a long tunnel. Apparently patients were ushered through this tunnel while priests above whispered words of encouragement and healing. A cool, refreshing breeze still blows through it offering relief from the sweltering summer sun. Galen, the famous doctor and anatomist, was born in Pergamum and practiced medicine in the Asclepieum.

The letter in Revelation"to the angel of the church at Pergamum" was from "the One who has the sharp, two-edged sword" (Revelation 2:12). He spoke of "the place where Satan has his throne" (Revelation 2:13). This might be the Altar of Zeus on the citadel; it is more likely that it refers to the fact that city was the center of Roman authority for the area and therefore the place of persecution for those who refused to worship Caesar.

In addition to this danger from the State there was the subtler temptation within the church itself from those people holding to the teaching of Balaam and to the doctrine of the Nicolatians (Revelation 2:14, 15). John told the church that the vision he saw threatened to "make war upon them with the sword that comes out of my mouth" (Revelation 2:16). But to those who repented and were victorious, "I will give some of the hidden manna; I will give him also a white stone, and on the stone will be written a new name, known to none but him that receives it" (Revelation 2:17). This last sounds like the promise of an amulet or talisman for protection here and immortality to come.

131

THYATIRA — AKHİSAR

Akhisar, the site of ancient Thyatira, is a thriving modern city, but with almost no remains of its old self to be seen except the ruins of an ancient temple, possibly to Apollo, a colonnaded road, and a large church. The city is on the main road between İzmir and Bursa, a road which runs somewhat parallel to the coast road from İzmir to Bergama. Akhisar lies in the valley of the Lycus (Kum Çayı) River (not to be confused with the Lycus near Laodicea), one of the chief tributaries of the Hermus (Gediz) River.

According to Pliny the Younger, Thyatira was founded by the Lydians and was called Pelopia. In the third century B.C. Seleucus Nicator took Lydia and garrisoned the place with Macedonian troops, renaming it Thyatira (town of Thya). Lysimachus, another of Alexander's generals, was then in control of Pergamum. Thyatira was on the border of both empires; first one side held it and then the other. In 190 B.C. Pergamum took it and strengthened it as a protection against the Seleucids of Sardis and beyond. A less defensible city is hard to imagine, lying as it does among softly rolling hills with only a bump for an acropolis. But it became an important outpost for the protection of Pergamum and Sardis, two of the world's greatest capitals at different times.

The coins of the ancient town give us clues to the kind of gods worshipped there. The chief god apparently was the sun god, Apollo-Tyrimnos, portrayed wearing only a cloak fastened with a brooch under his chin and carrying a battle-axe over his shoulder. Another coin shows the god astride a horse ready to go forth to battle. The military character of the city is well attested in these coins. After 132 B.C. when Roman influence became stronger, emperor worship was a part of Thyatiran ritual and the emperor was identified as Apollo incarnate.

The quality of the ruins that are still visible in Thyatira suggests that many more must be just under the surface. This is true also in other places in the Near East. But the values of uncovering them for the purposes of studying the past life of Akhisar and of attracting more sightseers to the town have to be weighed against the many questions of what likelihood there is of finding anything significant either to tourists or historians, of exposing the ruins to the even more ruinous pollution of today's air, and of disturbing people in homes and businesses who have a more immediate and active emotional attachment to the land than to history.

Josephus tells us that Seleucus probably settled a colony of Jews in Thyatira early in his rule, knowing that a garrison of soldiers alone could not produce a viable community. This is substantiated by inscriptions indicating the many trade guilds in the city. Even informal scratchings on theater seats or city pavements have provided archeologists with details of life 2000 years ago, and perhaps should give us pause in our annoyance at the quantities of red paint splashed across walls today. (Could it be that "Amerika" might be discovered 2000 years hence because of some leftist or rightest slogan still intact on a university building?)

No other city seems to have had so many guilds as Thyatira: coppersmiths, bronze workers, tanners, leather workers, dyers, workers in wool and linen, potters, bakers, and slave dealers. A member of one of these, Lydia of Thyatira, whom Paul met outside the city of Philippi (Acts 16:14) was a seller of purple goods. These may have been woolen and linen dyed Tyrian purple — a deep crimson made from snails and so expensive that robes of this material were worn as a mark of royalty. In Byzantine times "born in the purple" (porphyrogenitus) was the title of the son born after his father ascended the throne. Although snails are no longer used for this dye, in the Roman Catholic Church the phrase "promotion to the purple" still indicates elevation to the rank of cardinal. Lydia, as a trader in this cloth, must have been a person of some means. She was a worshipper of God and apparently a Gentile who had been attracted to Judaism in Thyatira.

In the first sentence of the letter in Revelation to the angel of the church in Thyatira there is a reference to "the Son of God, whose eyes flame like fire and whose feet gleam like burnished brass" (Revelation 2:18). Was John here comparing Christ with the emperor of Rome, who as the incarnate sun god Apollo was the son of Zeus? The word translated "burnished brass" is used nowhere else in the New Testament; it is one that the guild of bronze workers would recognize.

133

The members of the church of Thyatira were commended for doing more than they did at first (Revelation 2:19). However the fact that they made no effort to control the prophetess Jezebel was a cause of concern (Revelation 2:20). Jezebel was probably either a pseudonym or a general reference to licentiousness. The original Jezebel was a Phoenician Baal-worshipper and wife of Ahab, King of Israel. She left behind her a name for "obscene idol worship and monstrous sorceries" (II Kgs. 9:22).

Libertinism has been a constant threat to the Christian church. Had the followers of Jesus compromised with their non-Christian friends, the Christian group would have sunk and been engulfed by paganism. The threat to the church here was not from outside the church, not from emperor-worship or persecution, but from within in indulgence and lack of moral responsibility: "I am the searcher of men's hearts and thoughts" (Revelation 2:23). But to those who hold fast, "I will give authority over the nations... and I will give him also the star of dawn" (i.e., immortality) (Revelation 2:26, 28).

SARDIS — SART

One of the most picturesque areas of any of the Seven Churches is the site of Sardis. The spur of Mt. Tmolus (Boz Dağı) protrudes from the base of the mountain like the prow of a ship and constitutes the nigh impregnable citadel of the once famous city. Down through the ages wind and water have carved the sandstone and conglomerate of that spur and the surrounding country into distinctive sharp hills.

At the beginning of Sardian history (perhaps in the thirteenth century B.C.) the city occupied only the citadel. Centuries later the top of the spur proved too small, and thus a second city grew up around the base of the fortress. Together they became the center of one of the greatest kingdoms of the ancient world, Lydia. One of the kings of this period is Gyges, known to the Assyrians as Gugu, who sent ambassadors to Ashurbanipal (Sardanapalus), King of Assyria.

The famous temple of Artemis lying along the Pactolus (Sart Çayı) River dates from the fourth century B.C. Before that King Croesus (570-546 B.C.) built a temple there to Cybele between the river and the citadel. This temple was destroyed in 498 B.C. by an Athenian army during the revolt of the Ionian Confederacy against their Persian rulers. On the orders of Alexander the Great in 334 B.C. a new temple, this time to Artemis, was erected on the same site. Although the earlier temple was gone, the spirit of Cybele lived on and even invested the maiden Artemis with characteristics and practices of the Cybeline fertility cult.

Herodotus overflows with legends mixed with history when he writes about Sardis. He tell of Croesus who was the richest of men and lived behind what he thought were impregnable walls. All the sages of Greece, and among them Solon the wise, the reformer, the poet of Athens, came to see the great city of Sardis and its mighty king. Croesus lodged Solon in the royal palace and took him to ogle at his bulging treasuries.

When Solon had seen them all Croesus said, "Stranger of Athens, we have heard much of thy wisdom and of thy travels through many lands, from love of knowledge and a wish to see the world. I am curious therefore to inquire of thee, whom, of all the men that thou hast seen, thou deemest the most happy?" Thinking himself to be the happiest, Croesus was astonished that Solon selected someone else. Solon not only named Tellus of Athens but went on to give Croesus a lecture on wealth: "I see that thou art wonderfully rich, and art the lord of many nations; but with respect to that whereon thou questionest me, I have no answer to give, until I hear that thou hast closed thy life happily. For assuredly he who possesses great store of riches is no nearer happiness than he who has what suffices for his daily needs, unless it so hap that luck attend upon him, and so he continue in the enjoyment of all his good things to the end of life."*

135

Croesus is given the credit for improving the currency of the day. Up until his time the metal that was used in exchange had to be weighed for each transaction. Croesus minted pure gold and pure silver coins which were guaranteed at their face value by the state. This government currency made commerce more efficient and in so doing also helped finance art and literature.

Sardis was not impregnable, however. In the war between Croesus and the Persian Cyrus, Cyrus won the first round of the battle by a ruse that only an Eastern general would think of. That was based on the knowledge that horses greatly dislike the sight and smell of camels. Thus when Cyrus saw the army of Croesus arranged on the plain before the city he ordered all the baggage-carrying camels to be unloaded and his horsemen to mount these beasts and thus attack the cavalry of the Lydians. The horses, as he had expected, turned and fled, and the unmounted soldiers retreated behind the safe walls of the citadel.

In the fourteenth day of the seige that followed, Cyrus offered a reward to the first Persian soldier who would climb the precipitous wall. The Mardian Hyroeades had seen a Lydian accidentally drop his helmet over the wall of the fortress on its steepest side and later climb down the rock to recover it. Hyroeades the following night took a band of fellow soldiers and cautiously climbed the precipice from crevice to crevice to the top as he had seen the Lydian do. Because the Lydians thought this part of the wall was inaccessible there were no defenders there

* Herodotus, Book I, chaps. 29-32.

and so Sardis fell to the Persians and the reign of Croesus came to an end in 546 B.C.

Croesus was captured and about to be burned alive when Cyrus heard him saying, "Solon, Solon, Solon." That provoked Cyrus's curiosity, The fire was put out (Heredotus says by supernatural intervention), and Croesus was asked to explain what Solon had said about judging a man's happiness before his life was finished. As the two kings were conversing, Croesus asked Cyrus what his soldiers were doing. "Plundering thy city, and carrying off thy riches," answered Cyrus. "Not my city," said Croesus, "nor my riches. They are not mine any more, It is thy wealth which they are pillaging." Cyrus promptly stopped the raid.*

Perhaps one of the reasons that there are so many incidents reported about Croesus is because he had a good story-teller in residence in his court. It is said that Aesop was a Phrygian who lived in Sardis at this time.

Besides the temple, a small Byzantine church on one corner, and the acropolis (which few people have the interest or the stamina to explore), recent excavations have uncovered a synagogue, the last several meters of the Royal Road from Susa to Sardis, a number of shops, and the gymnasium. The gymnasium and the synagogue have been partially restored. Important finds from this area are in the museum in Manisa.

John told the Christians of Sardis that the letter in Revelation was from "the One who holds the seven spirits of God, the seven stars" (Revelation 3:1). He admonished them to, "Wake up, and put some strength into what is left" (Revelation 3:2). The church probably appeared prosperous and active as do many of today's large congregations. But to John the outward seeming did not tally with the finished work: "... though you have a name for being alive, you are dead... For I have not found any work of yours completed in the eyes of my God" (Revelation 3:1-2). To those on the other hand who were innocent of pollution he promised that they shall walk

136

Op.cit.chaps. 88-90.

with Christ "robed all in white" (Revelation 3:5), the color of righteousness and immortality. In each of the letters John offered a specific reward that would assure the faithful of blessedness and eternal life.

PHILADELPHIA — ALAŞEHİR

Philadelphia was the least distinguished of the cities of the Seven Churches. It was the latest to take on importance as a city, and only a few ruins are visible now. However, on the positive side, it was located on the outer edge of Hellenistic civilization and the Christian faith, and therefore had grave responsibilities for spreading the thought patterns and activities of these transforming powers. Furthermore, Philadelphia and Smyrna were the only two churches among the Seven about which nothing bad was said by John.

Ancient Philadelphia, the city of brotherly love, is now called Alaşehir. It is located about forty-five kilometers southeast of Sardis and on the northeast edge of Boz Dağı. There was a citadel above the town which would have offered some resistance to invaders but was not as easily defended as that at Sardis. On the lower sides of the city are sections of thick Byzantine walls which served as an outer defense in the Middle Ages.

The most interesting remains of Christian Philadelphia are in the Beş Eylûl area of the city. They consist of part of a Byzantine basilica built of brick, with a bit of high arch and some eleventh century frescoes in very poor condition that are exposed to the elements. From what is left it is difficult to judge the value of the original or the importance of trying to preserve it.

Philadelphia was founded in the reign of Attalus II, Philadelphus of Pergamum, when a group of Macedonian soldiers were sent to occupy this strategic hill as an outpost of the Pergamene kingdom. Attalus was given the title "Philadelphus" because of his loyal love for his brother Eumenes, who preceded him as king. The coins of this period show two identical brothers.

Calletebus, the Lydian name for the town, had been occupied for centuries before it was developed by the

Pergamenes. It lay on the Persian Royal Road and controlled two of the most important valleys of western Asia Minor, the Hermus (Gediz) and the Meander (Menderes) Rivers. It was near the ascent to the pass into the high central plateau of Phrygia. Ramsay says that the intention of the founder of Philadelphia was to make it the center of a Greco-Asiatic culture and a means of spreading the Greek language and manners into eastern Lydia and Phrygia. By 19 A.D. the Lydian tongue had ceased to be spoken in Lydia, and Greek was the language of the country.

Philadelphia (as well as Sardis) lies in an area of western Turkey where there have been frequent earthquakes. It was destroyed in 17 and in 23 A.D., but rebuilt through the generosity of the Roman Emperor, Tiberius.

Religion in Philadelphia before the Christian era revolved around the gods of Olympus and the local gods more than around the emperor-gods of the Romans. The people of Pergamum worshipped Zeus and the emperor-god, Trajan, but their own local healer-god, Asclepius, came before either Zeus or the emperor. Although Philadelphia was tied administratively to Pergamum, since it was a center for the cultivation of the grape, the main god was naturally Dionysus. We find inscriptions connected with Dionysus which speak of confession of sin, punishment of sin by the god, and thanks to him also. Now Alaşehir is a center for harvesting licorice along with the grapes.

From its beginning as an outpost of Pergamum, Philadelphia was a missionary city. In the beginning it witnessed to Hellenistic culture and language among the people living east of Lydia. In Christian times it witnessed to non-Christians on the fringe of the Christian world.

John perhaps was using that theme when he said in Revelation,"These are words of the holy one, the true one, who holds the key of David;... I have set before you an open door, which no one can shut" (Revelation 3:7-8). Perhaps the open door was the opportunity for missionary work beyond the pass into Phrygia; perhaps it was to the new Jerusalem because of the obedience of the

Philadelphians. Or perhaps it was the door that opened into the limitless challenge and opportunity of Christian life.

John warned that the whole world would shortly face an ordeal to test its inhabitants. He noted that the church was not strong but that the members were loyal. "Hold fast to what you have, and let no one rob you of your crown," he advised (Revelation 3:11). John promised that the victorious, on the second coming, will be "a pillar in the temple of my God;... I will write the name of my God upon him, and the name of the city of my God, that new Jerusalem..." (Revelation 3:12).

139

LAODICEA — LAODİKEA

The present-day visitor to Laodicea finds a large area littered with broken marble, tops of stone masonry walls, and here and there public buildings: two theaters, a large stadium, nearby it a water tower, an odeon, and the nymphaeum which was excavated in 1961-1963. In the side of the hill just as one approaches Laodicea one can also see the truncated conduits that were part of the water supply system for the city. Much, much more is obviously right under foot.

Laodicea's origins, as far as are presently known, go back to one of the Hellenistic kings in the middle of the third century B.C. It is supposed to have been named or renamed then by Antiochus II in honor of his wife, Laodicea, but the origins must go back earlier. Cicero lived in Laodicea in the early months of 50 B.C. administering justice and trying to make up for the distress caused throughout the province by his predecessor, Appius Claudius. One of the requests Cicero turned down at this time was that of sending wild animals to his friends for their games in Rome. (Incidentally, Cicero's letters are a most fruitful source for details on life and personalities of his time.)

The city was at the crossroads of north-south traffic between Sardis and Perga and east-west traffic from the Euphrates to Ephesus. Laodicea quickly became a rich city, rich enough to be able to rebuild itself without outside help after the destructive earthquake of 60 A.D. In common with many of the Hellenistic cities there was a prosperous Jewish colony established there well before the Christian era. The city's reputation was for its money transactions and the good quality of raven-black wool grown in the area. Many of the coins were stamped with the image of Zeus Azeus, the main god of the city and possibly the god of a temple there dating before Antiochus.

140

About twenty kilometers west of Laodicea, where the Lycus (Çürüksu) River passes through the Phrygian Gate there used to be a famous temple to Men Karou. Strabo reports, "Between Laodicea and Carura is a temple of Men Carus which is held in remarkable veneration. In my own time a great... school of medicine has been established. A market was also held there under the protection of the god."*

One of the principles of medicine at that time was that compound diseases required compound medicines. One of the compounds used for strengthening the ears was made from the spice nard (spikenard? an aromatic plant). Galen says that it was originally made only in Laodicea, although by the second century A.D. it was made in other places also. Galen also described a medicine for the eyes made of Phrygian stone. Aristotle spoke of it as a Phrygian powder. Ramsay tries to explain what kind of medicine it was by saying it was not an ointment but a cylindrical collyrium that could be powdered and then spread on the part affected. The term used by John in Revelation is the same that Galen uses to describe the preparation of the Phrygian stone.** Would not these medicinal concoctions be a reason why John cautions the Laodiceans to buy "ointment for your eyes so that you may see" (Revelation 3:18)?

Possibly John had the springs of Hierapolis (Pamukkale) which was just across the valley from Laodicea in mind when he said, "I know all your ways; you are neither hot nor cold. How I wish you were either hot or cold! But because you are lukewarm, neither hot nor

---

* Strabo, **The Geography of Strabo**, vol. 5, 519
** Ramsey, **The Letters to the Seven Churches of Asia**, p.429.

cold, I will spit you out of my mouth" (Revelation 3:15-17)! This abhorrence of those who refused to commit themselves utterly to their faith helped preserve the early church.

John promised in "the words of the Amen" (Revelation 3:14) that for those who were sensitive enough to hear and respond to what was being said, the Spirit would join them in the great feast. "Here I stand knocking at the door; if anyone hears my voice and opens the door, I will come in and sit down to supper with him and he with me" (Revelation 3:20). John concluded this series of letters to the Seven Churches with an even more attractive promise from the Spirit: "To him who is victorious I will grant a place on my throne, as I myself was victorious and sat down with my Father on his throne" (Revelation 3:21).

141

CONCLUSION

The fascination which many people feel in the physical and geographical surroundings of past events can be richly rewarded in Turkey. So many places here echo through our backgrounds and arouse our emotional identification with one group or another who have lived here; so many of our concepts of history, geometry, physics, philosophy, and, supremely, worship can be given a tangible birthplace. But let us not transgress in a wrongful pride of ownership.

Still it is appropriate in a trip through Turkey to find increased appreciation of our heritage and respect for the quality of those who have walked this land before us. This book has attempted to describe some of the situations and some of the people important in the area and in events reported in the Bible. In this the interpretation is basically historical. This does not mean to negate the inspired message, but rather to help give us a framework in which that can be applied to our lives today.

While events reported in the New Testament are considerably more immediate to our lives than those in the early parts of the Old Testament, they also sometimes have details that are no longer applicable in our exercise of our faith. The concerns and understanding of the early Christian Fathers have been modified in the flow of world events: John's anti-semitism in the letters to the churches of Smyrna and Philadelphia can be understood as an outcome of discrimination between the Jews who were exempt from worshipping Roman gods and the Christians who were persecuted because they refused polytheism. But the fact that John felt the injustice then does not today excuse our continuing to the cherish this hatred.

Other details also identify the books of the New Testament with the early centuries of Christianity: slow travel and communication, references to places that no longer exist and acceptance of customs such as slavery that are condemned today. The current issues of outer space, ecology, nuclear physics, finite energy, industrialization, and biological and economic interdependence of nations, to name only a few, point to some of the changes in our conceptions of the world that have taken place in these intervening years. These differences, however, do not touch the essential validity of God's imperative to us.

144

As the book of Genesis has to do with the ideas of our beginnings and our relations with God, so the Book of Revelation concerns God's judgments and our finalities. Throughout the Bible there is a stern awareness of the realities of human existence and the uncompromising demands of the discipline of worship of God. The references in the New Testament to the early church show the struggle its members had to know where they were going and to maintain that discipline. Paul, John, Polycarp, Basil, and all the rest were trying with all their minds to strengthen the small group who could easily have been discouraged and have died out. They must often have been discouraged themselves in the cycle of honor and then martyrdom for the loyal followers of Christ. But for all of the seductive evil which the Bible acknowledges and the fearsome awe without which God cannot be worshipped, the Bible is a joyous, triumphant book. The message of the Book throughout is one for all of us, irrespective of our position, our learning, our abilities. Although it takes us all our lives to understand it, the message of Revelation 22:17 is simple and direct:

" 'Come!' say the Spirit and the bride.
" 'Come!' let each hearer reply.
"Come forward, you who are thirsty; accept the water of life, a free gift to all who desire it."

Antalya harbor

Kaleköy near Kekova

Fethiye: islands

Myra: Church of St. Nicholas

PAUL'S JOURNEYS

Suggested Dates

EARLY YEARS

Native of Tarsus (Acts 22:3)	
Jerusalem (study under Gamaliel, Acts 22 : 3)	
Damascus (vision on the road; conversion, Acts 9:3 ff.)	33 A.D.
Arabia: (withdrawal, Galatians 1:17)	
Damascus (escaped in a basket, Acts 9:25)	
Jerusalem (met Peter and James, Galatians 1:18-19)	35
Caesarea of Phoenicia (port of embarcation)	
Tarsus (preaching, Acts 9:30; Galatians 1:23)	
Syria and Cilicia (Galatians 1:21)	
Antioch (with Barnabas, Acts 11:25-26)	43
Jerusalem? (private interview; circumcision of Titus? Galatians 2:1)	
Antioch?	
Jerusalem (carried relief funds, Acts 11:30; or same trip as Galatians 2:1)	

FIRST MISSIONARY JOURNEY (Acts 13:4-14:28)	47-49
Antioch	46? 47?
Seleucia (with Barnabas and John Mark, Acts 12:25)	47
Cyprus	
Salamis (Acts 13:5)	
Paphos (preaching to proconsul Sergius Paulus and others, Acts 13:6 ff.)	
Pamphylia	
Attalia?, Side?	
Perga (John Mark leaves; Paul sick? Acts 13:13; Galatians 4:13)	
Antioch of Pisidia (Acts 13:14)	fall 46? 47?
Iconium (Paul and Barnabas escaped maltreatment, Acts 14:5-6)	
Lystra (Barnabas thought to be Jupiter, Paul Mercury, Acts 14:12)	
Derbe (Acts 14:20)	
Attalia (port of departure, Acts 14:26)	
Antioch (Paul and Peter at odds, Galatians 2:11 ff.)	49? 50?

BIBLICAL SITES IN TURKEY

CONFERENCE IN JERUSALEM (Acts 15:1-29)

Phoenicia (Acts 15:3)
Samaria
Jerusalem (apostolic council concerning circum-
cision vs. power of Holy Spirit, Acts 15 : 4 ff.)   49? 50?

SECOND MISSIONARY JOURNEY (Acts 15:36-
18:22)   50-53

146

Antioch (Paul and Silas together: Barnabas with
John Mark to Cyprus, Acts 15:39)   50
Syria and Cilicia (Acts 15:41)
Derbe (Acts 16:1)
Lystra (Timothy joins Paul, Acts 16:1 ff.)
Phrygia, Galatia (Paul turned aside from Asia
and Bithynia, Acts 16:7; Iconium? An-
tioch? Tavium? Ancyra? Pessinus?)
Mysia
Alexandria Troas (Luke joined group; Paul
dreamt of Macedonian calling him, Acts
16:9)
Samothrace (Acts 16:11)
Macedonia
Neapolis
Philippi (lodged with Lydia of Thyatira;
Paul freed from prison by earthquake,
Acts 16:12-40)
Amphipolis (Acts 17:1)
Apollonia
Thessalonica (trouble with Jews, Acts 17:1
ff.)
Beroea (Silas and Timothy left there Acts
17:10-14)
Athens (Paul addressed Court of Areopagus,
Acts 17:22 ff.)
Corinth (Silas and Timothy rejoined Paul; worked
with Aquila and Priscilla as tentmakers; first
missionary letters? I Thessalonians 3:1; Acts 18:1 ff.)
Cenchreae (Paul shaved his head, Acts 18:18)
Ephesus (Paul left Aquila and Priscilla, continued to
Caesarea, Acts 18:19)
Syria
Caesarea of Phoenicia
Jerusalem (Acts 18:22)
Antioch (Timothy joined Paul?)

PAUL'S JOURNEYS

THIRD MISSIONARY JOURNEY (Acts 18:23-21:17)   53-57

Galatia, Phrygia (Acts 18:23; 19:1; Tavium?
    Ancyra? Pessinus? or Derbe? Lystra?
    Iconium?)
Ephesus (Paul spent 2 1/4 years; riot of
    silversmiths, Acts 19:10, 23-41)
Overland to Macedonia (Acts 20:2; Smyrna?
    Pergamum? Adramyttium?)
Alexandria Troas? (Paul preached successfully,
    II Corinthians 2:12)
Macedonia (Titus joined Paul in Macedonia, II   147
    Corinthians 7:6) Philippi? Amphipolis?
    Thessalonica? Beroea?
Dyrrhachium? (Acts 20:2)
Apollonia? Nicopolis? Athens?
Corinth (Paul here three months; heard of
    plot against his life, Acts 20:3)
Cenchreae
Macedonia
    Philippi (Paul spent Passover; sailed with
        Luke, Acts 20:6)
    Neapolis
Troas (Eutychus fell out of window, Acts 20:9)
Assos (Paul joined ship from Troas, Acts 20:13)
Mytilene (Acts 20:14)
Chios
Erythrea? (Acts 20:15)
Samos
Trogillium (KJV, Acts 20:15)
Miletus (Paul preached to presbyters of Ephesus,
    Acts 20:15 ff.)
Cos (Acts 21:1)
Rhodes
Patara
Tyre (Acts 21:3)
Ptolemais (Acts 21:7)
Caesarea of Phoenicia (party stayed with Philip,
    Acts 21:8)
Jerusalem (Paul received by James, Acts 21:18)

JOURNEY TO ROME (Acts 27:1-28:15)   59? 60?

Jerusalem (riot in Temple causing Paul's arrest,
    Acts 21:27 ff.)   57
Caesarea of Phoenicia (Paul under Roman guard
    two years for protection, Acts 24:27)
Sidon (Luke and Aristarchus accompanied Paul
    with centurion Julius, Acts 27:2)
Myra (transship to vessel for Italy, Acts 27:6)
Cnidus (too stormy to land, Acts 27:7)

Fair Haven (Acts 27:8)
Cauda (Acts 27:16)
Malta (shipwrecked, Acts 27:39 ff.)
Syracuse (Acts 28:12)
Rhegium
Puteoli (Acts 28:13)
Appii Forum, Three Taverns (Christians of
   Rome met party, Acts 28:15)
Rome (Paul lived two years in hired house, Acts
   28:30)   60?

148

OTHER TRAVELS?

Crete? (Titus 1:5)
Illyricum? (Romans 15:19)
Spain? (Romans 15:24)
Corinth? (II Timothy 4:20)
Ephesus? Miletus?

DEATH

Martyrdom in Rome   62? 64? 67?

COMPARATIVE LIST OF PLACE NAMES

The historical or common English name is given first, followed by the Turkish name. In parentheses the location of the place on the map or maps at the front of the book is indicated.

A

Adramyttium, between Edremit and Burhaniye (I B1, III A2)
Aegean Sea, Ege Denizi (I A2-5, II A1-3, III A2-3)
————— Alaca Höyük (II C1)
Aleppo, Halep (II C3)
Alexandretta, İskenderun (II C2, III D3)
Alexandria Troas, Eski İstanbul, near Odun İskelesi (I A1, III A2)
Amastris, Amasra (III C1)
Amisus, Samsun (II C1, III D1)
Anatolia, Anadolu (I, II, III)
Ancyra, Ankara (II B2, III C2)

Anemurium, Anamur (III C3)
Antioch of Pisidia, Yalvaç (III B2)
Antioch-on-the-Orontes, Antakya (II C3, III D3)
Aphrodisias, Geyre (III B3)
Aram (II D2)
Ararat, Büyük Ağrı Dağı (II E2)
Araxes River, Aras (II D-F2)
Ashkenaz (II E1)
Asia (III A2)
Aspendos, Aspendos, Balkır (III B3)
Asshur (II D2)
Assos, Makhramion, Behramkale (1 A1, III A2)
Attalia, Antalya (III B3)
Axylon, Cihanbeyli Yaylası (III C2)

B

————— Baku (II F1)
Barbysus, Kağıthane Suyu
————— Beldibi (II B2)
Birtha, Birecik (II D2)
Bithynia (III B2)
Black Sea, Kara Deniz (II B-D1, III B-D1)

BIBLICAL SITES IN TURKEY

Bosphorus, İstanbul Boğazı (II B1, III B1)
Bulgaria, Bulgaristan (III A1)
Byzantium, İstanbul (II B1, III B1)

C

Caesarea Mazaca, Kayseri (III D2)
Caicus River, Şakır Çayı
Calletebus, Philadelphia, Alaşehir (I E3, III B2)
Calycadnus River, Göksü (III C3)
Cappadocia, (III C-D 2-3)
Carchemish, Karkemiş, Barak (II C2, III D3)
Caria (III A3)
Caspian Sea, Hazar Denizi (II F 1-2)
Cayster River Küçük Menderes
Cestrus River, Aksu
Chalcedon, Kadıköy (III B1)
Chios, Sakız (II A2, III A2)
Cilicia (III C3)
Cilician Gates, Gülek Boğazı (III C3)
Claros, Ahmetbeyli (I C4)
Claudiopolis, Mut (III C3)
Clazomene, north of Urla (I B3)
Cnidus, Knidos, Datça (III A3)
Coa (II C2)
Colophon, Değirmendere (I C4)
Colossae, near Honaz (III B3)
Commagene (III D3)
Constantinople, İstanbul (II B1, III B1)
Cos, İstanköy Adası (II A2, III A3)
Cotyaeum, Kütahya (III B2)
Cydnus River, Tarsus Suyu (III C3)
Cyprus, Kıbrıs (II B-C3, III C4)
Cyzicus, Erdek III A1)
　　　　　Çatal Höyük (II B2)

D

Dardanelles, Çanakkale Boğazı (II A1, III A1-2)
Danunas, Adana (II C2, III D3)
Derbe, Kerti Höyük?, Unu Höyük?, Aşıran Höyük? Değle? (III C3)
Didyma, Didim. Yenihisar (III A3)
──────── Doğubayazıt (II E2)
Dorylaeum, Eskişehir (III B2)

E

Edessa, Urfa (II D2)
Ephesus, Efes (I C4, III A2)
Erythrea, Ildır (I A3)
──────── Erzincan (II D2)

COMPARATIVE LIST

—————— Erzurum (II D2)
Euphrates River, Fırat (II D-E2-3, III D3-4)

G

Galatia (III C2)
Gangra, Çankırı (II C1, III C2)
—————— Gevaş (II E2)
Gog (II E1)
Gomer (II D1)
Gordium, Gordion (II B2, III C2)
Granicus, north of Biga (III A2)
Greece, Yunanistan (III A1)
Gulf of Cos, Kerme Körfezi (1 C-D5, III A3)
Gulf of Heracleia, Bafa Gölü (I C4-5)
—————— Gürün (III D2)

H

Halicarnassus, Bodrum (I C5, III A3)
Halys River, Kızılırmak (II C1-2, III C-D1-2)
Harran, Carrhae, Altınbaşak (II D2)
Hattusas, Boğazkale (II C2, III C2)
Heracleia, Kapı Kırık Yaylası (I C4)
Hermus River, Gediz (1 B-E 3, II A-B2, III A-B2)
Hermus River, Meriç
Hierapolis, Pamukkale (III B3)

I

Iconium, Konya (III C3)
Ilium, Truva (I A1, III A2)
Isauria (III C3)

J

Javan (II A1)

K

—————— Kale (II D2)
Kanesh, Nesa, Kültepe (II C2, III D2)
Karalis Lake, Beyşehir Gölü, (III B3)
—————— Keban (II D2)
Kizzuwatna (II C2)

L

Laodicea, Laodikea, near Goncalı (III B3)
Lebanon, Lübnan (III D4)
Lesbos, Mytilene, Midilli Adası (I A2, II A2, III A2)
Limnai Lake, Eğridir Gölü (III B2-3)

BIBLICAL SITES IN TURKEY

Lud (II A2)
Lycaonia (III C3)
Lycia (III B3)
Lycus River, tributary of Hermus, Kum Çayı
Lycus River, tributary of Meander, Çürüksu
Lydia (III A2)
Lygus, İstanbul (II B2, III B2)
Lysimachia, Ekzamíl (III A1)
Lystra, Gilistra? Ilıstra? (III C3)

M

Magnesia-on-the-Meander, Kemer, south of Ortaklar (I C4)
Magnesia-ad-Sipylum, Manisa (I C3)
Makhramion, Assos, Behramkale (I A1, III A2)
———————— Malatya (II D2)
Meander River, Büyük Menderes (I C-E4, II A-B2, III A-B2-3)
Media (II E2)
Mediterranean Sea, Akdeniz (II A-C3, III A-C4)
———————— Meryem Ana, near Ephesus
Meshech (II B2)
Miletus Milet, Balat (I C4, III A3)
Minni (II E2-3)
Mt. Ararat, Büyük Ağrı Dağı (II E2)
Mt. Argaeus, Erciyes Dağı (II C2, III*D2)
Mt. Cadus, Honaz Dağı (III B3)
Mt. Ida, Kaz Dağı (I B1, III A2)
Mt. Mycale, Samsun Dağı
Mt. Pagus, Kadifekalesi
Mt. Pieria, Musa Dağı
Mt. Olympus, Ulu Dağ (III B2)
Mt. Pion, Panayır Dağı
Mt. Sipylus, Manisa Dağı
Mt. Tmolus, Boz Dağ (III A2)
Mylassa, Milas (I D5)
Myra, Demre (III B3)
Mysia (III A2)
Mytilene, Midilli Adası (I A2, II A2, III A2)

N

Nicaea, İznik (III B2)
Nicomedia, İzmit (III B1)
Nineveh (II E3)

O

Olympos, Çıralı (III B3)
Orontes River, Âsi Irmak (II C3, III D3-4)

P

Pactolus River, Sart Çayı
———————— Palu (II D2)

COMPARATIVE LIST

Pamphylia (III B3)
Panionium, Davutlar (I C4)
Paphlagonia (III C1)
Patara, Gelemiş (III B3)
Patmos, Patmos Adası (III A3)
Pelopia, Thyatira, Akhisar (I D2, III A2)
Pergamum, Bergama (I C2, III A2)
Perga, Murtuna (III B3)
Pessinus, Ballıhisar (III B2)
Philadelphia, Alaşehir (I E3, III B2)
Phocea, Foça (I B3)
Phrygia (III B2) 153
Pisidia (III B3)
Pontus (III D2)
Priene, Güllübahçe (I C4, III A3)
Propontus, Marmara Denizi (III A-B1)
Prusa, Bursa (III B2)

R

Rhodes; Rodos (II A2, III A3)
Riphath (II B1)

S

Sagalassus, Ağlasun (III B3)
Samos, Sisam (I B4; II A2, III A3)
Samosata, Samsat (II D2)
Sangarius River, Sakarya Nehri (II B1-2, III B-C1-2)
Sarus River, Seyhan Nehri (III D3)
Sardis, Sart (I D3, III A2) ‚
Sebasteia, Sivas (II C2) ˈ
Seleucia of Isauria, Silifke (III C3)
Seleucia Pieria, Samandağ (III D3)
Selinus River, Bergama Çayı
Semistra, İstanbul (II B2, III B2)
Sepharad (II A2)
Side, Side (III B3)
Sinope, Sinop (II C1, III D1)
Smyrna, İzmir (I C3, II A2, III A2)
Soandos, Nevşehir (III C2)
Soli (III C3)
Syria Suriye (III D4)

T

Tarshish (II B3)
Tarsus, Tarsus (II C2, III C3)
Tatta Lake, Tuz Gölü (III C2)
Taurus Mountains, Toros Dağları (II B-C2)
Tavium, Büyük Nefes Köy? (III C2)
Tegarama, Gürün (II C2, III D2)

Telmessus, Fethiye (III B3)
Teos, Sığacık (I B3)
Termessus (III B3)
Thrace, Trakya (III A1)
Thyatira, Akhisar (I D2, III A2)
Tigris River, Dicle (II D-E2-3)
Togarmah, Gürün (II C2, III D2)
Trajanopolis, Uşak (III B2)
Trapezus, Trabzon (II D1)
Trogillium, Dip Burnu (I B4)
Troy, Ilium, Truva (I A1, III A2)
Tubal (II C2)
Tushpa, Van (II E2)

U

Urmia Lake, Urmiye Gölü (II E2)
———— Ürgüp (III D2)

V

———— Van (II E2)
Van Lake, Van Gölü (II E2)

X

Xanthos, Kınık (III B3)
Xanthos River, Kocaçay

Z

Zagros Mountains (II E-F3)

Appendix 3

SUGGESTED TOURS

The itineraries suggested here among biblical and historical sites in Turkey are given with the assumption that the sightseer has the use of an automobile. A good road map (available from the Turkish Ministry of Tourism and Information), a good recent guidebook for Turkey, and a Bible are also recommended for these trips. Contrary to the rest of the book, the names here are given insofar as possible as they appear on the Turkish road map.

The numbers of days indicated for each tour or individual site are based on two objectives: to enable the tourist to see the site as a nonspecialist would want, and to arrive conveniently at the most, comfortable place in the area for spending the night. Hotels vary in their splendor, but even the plainest are generally adequate for a night or two. The trips are planned for summer daylight.

Itinerary I: İstanbul to İzmir and Ankara and back, 7 days

Ist day: İstanbul to Çanakkale and Troy

İstanbul to Keşan	223 km.	
Keşan to Eceabat	121 km.	
Eceabat to Çanakkale	2 km.	
(allow time for ferry)		
Çanakkale to Troy and back	62 km.	408 km.

2nd day: Çanakkale to İzmir

Çanakkale to Alexandria Troas	67 km.	
Alexandria Troas to Behramköy	62 km.	
Behramköy to Bergama	185 km.	
Bergama to İzmir	105 km.	419 km.

3rd day: İzmir

4th day: İzmir to Efes and Meryem Ana and back	180 km.

5th day: İzmir to Afyon

İzmir to Sart	100 km.	
Sart to Alaşehir	58 km.	
Alaşehir to Afyon	210 km.	368 km.

6 th day: Afyon to Ankara	257 km.

7 th day: Ankara to İstanbul (via Bolu)	438 km.

BIBLICAL SITES IN TURKEY

Itinerary II: The Seven Churches, 5 days

1st day: İzmir

2nd day: İzmir to Efes and Meryem Ana and back   180 km.

3rd day: İzmir to Akhisar and Bergama and back

İzmir to Akhisar	95 km.	
Akhisar to Bergama	85 km.	
Bergama to İzmir	105 km.	285 km.

4th day: İzmir to Laodikea

İzmir to Sart	100 km.	
Sart to Alaşehir	58 km.	
Alaşehir to Laodikea	110 km.	
Laodikea to Pamukkale	10 km.	278 km.

5th day: Pamukkale to İzmir

Pamukkale to Colossae (Honaz)	30 km.	
Colossae to Geyre (Aphrodisias)	113 km.	
Geyre to İzmir	179 km.	321 km.

Itinerary III: İstanbul to Antakya via Ağrı Dağı, 12 Days

1st day: İstanbul to Ankara via Bolu   438 km.

or: İstanbul to Ankara via Eskişehir

İstanbul to Eskişehir	315 km.	
Eskişehir to Ballıhisar	67 km.	
Ballıhisar to Gordion	54 km.	
Gordion to Ankara	103 km.	539 km.

2nd day: Ankara

3rd day: Ankara to Sungurlu

Ankara to Boğazkale	197 km.	
Boğazkale to Alaca Höyük	33 km.	
Alaca Höyük to Sungurlu	37 km.	267 km.

4th day: Sungurlu to Samsun

Sungurlu to Merzifon	136 km.	
Merzifon to Amasya	47 km.	
Amasya to Samsun	128 km.	311 km.

SUGGESTED TOURS

5th day: Samsun to Trabzon
    Samsun to Ordu   164 km.
    Ordu to Giresun   47 km.
    Giresun to Trabzon   150 km.   361 km.

6th day: Trabzon to Erzurum
    Trabzon to Maçka   21 km.
    Maçka to Sumela and back   44 km.
    Maçka to Gümüşhane   88 km.
    Gümüşhane to Erzurum   206 km.   359 km.

7th day: Erzurum to Doğubayazıt and Ağrı
    Erzurum to Ağrı   189 km.
    Ağrı to Doğubayazıt and back   192 km.   381 km.

(If Ağrı Dağı is cloud-covered you may want to repeat the trip to Doğubayazıt early the next morning.)

8th day: Ağrı to Van
    Ağrı to Van   230 km.
    Van to Ahtamar and back   60 km.   290 km.

9th day: Van to Diyarbakır
    Van to Bitlis   175 km.
    Bitlis to Diyarbakır   231 km.   406 km.

10th day: Diyarbakır to Gaziantep
    Diyarbakır to Urfa   184 km.
    Urfa to Altınbaşak and back   86 km.
    Urfa to Gaziantep   146 km.   416 km.

11th day: Gaziantep to Barak and back   154 km.

12th day: Gaziantep to Antakya   197 km.

(Without all of the side trips ten days are enough for this trip.)

BIBLICAL SITES IN TURKEY

Itinerary IV: Antakya to Antalya, 4 days

1st day: Antakya to Adana
Antakya to İskenderun	57 km.	
İskenderun to Toprakkale	55 km.	
Toprakkale, Misis, Yılankale to Adana	78 km.	190 km.

2nd day: Adana to Silifke
Adana to Tarsus	39 km.	
Tarsus to Soli	38 km.	
Soli to Kız Kalesi	52 km.	
Kız Kalesi to Cennet ve Cehennem	10 km.	
Cennet ve Cehennem to Silifke	26 km.	
Silifke to Ayatekla and back	2 km	167 km.

3rd day: Silifke to Alanya
Silifke to Anamur	138 km.	
Anamur to Alanya	128 km.	266 km.

4th day: Alanya to Antalya
Alanya to Manavgat	63 km.	
Manavgat to Side	7 km.	
Side to Aspendos	38 km.	
Aspendos to Perge	25 km.	
Perge to Antalya	15 km.	148 km.

Itinerary V: Antalya to Fethiye and back (Summer), 2 days

1st day: Antalya to Fethiye
Antalya to Kemer (Beldibi)	29 km.	
Kemer to Demre	133 km.	
Demre to Gelemiş	92 km.	
Gelemiş to Fethiye	61 km.	315 km.

2nd day: Fethiye to Antalya
Fethiye to Kaş	104 km.	
Kaş to Finike	79 km.	
Finike to Chimaera	58 km.	
Chimaera to Antalya	72 km.	313 km.

SUGGESTED TOURS

Itinerary VI: Antalya to İzmir, 3 days

Antalya to Termessos	25 km.	
1st day: Antalya to Pamukkale		
Termessos to Isparta	148 km.	
Isparta to Dinar	62 km.	
Dinar to Laodikea	112 km.	
Laodikea to Pamukkale	10 km.	357 km.

2nd day: Pamukkale to Aydın

159

Pamukkale to Colossae	30 km.	
Colossae to Denizli	25 km.	
Denizli to Geyre (Aphrodisias)	100 km.	
Geyre to Aydın	98 km.	253 km.

3rd day: Aydın to İzmir

Aydın to Selçuk	50 km.	
Selçuk to Efes	5 km.	
Efes to Meryem Ana	13 km.	
Meryem Ana to İzmir	81 km.	149 km.

Itinerary VII: Antalya to Konya via Yalvaç, 1 day

1st day: Antalya to Isparta	146 km.	
Isparta to Yalvaç	130 km.	
Yalvaç to Konya	187 km.	463 km.

Itinerary VIII: Konya to Adana, 3 days

1st day: Konya, Gilistra and Çatal Höyük

Konya to Gilistra and back	64 km.	
Konya to Çatal Höyük and back	114 km.	178 km.

2nd day: Konya to Aşıran Höyük and back	250 km.

3rd day: Konya to Adana (via Cilician Gates)	348 km.

BIBLICAL SITES IN TURKEY

Itinerary IX: Adana to Bursa via Konya and Kütahya, 2 days

1st day: Adana to Akşehir
Adana to Konya (via Silifke)	410 km.	
Konya to Akşehir	134 km.	544 km.

2nd day: Akşehir to Bursa
Akşehir to Afyon	94 km.	
Afyon to Kütahya	99 km.	
Kütahya to Bursa	190 km.	383 km.

Itinerary X: Ankara to Ürgüp and back, 2 days

1st day: Ankara to Ürgüp
Ankara to Kırşehir	192 km.	
Kırşehir to Nevşehir	92 km.	
Nevşehir to Göreme, Ürgüp and back	50 km.	334 km.

2nd day: Nevşehir to Ankara
Nevşehir to Derinkuyu and back	60 km.	
Nevşehir to Aksaray	79 km.	
Aksaray to Ihlara and back (summer)	64 km.	
Aksaray to Ankara	223 km.	426 km.

BIBLIOGRAPHY

Akurgal, Ekrem, **Ancient Civilizations and Ruins of Turkey,** Mobil Oil Türk A.Ş., İstanbul, 1969.

Alkım, U. Bahadır, **Anatolia I,** Nagel Publishers, Geneva, 1968.

Anatolian Studies, Journal of the British Institute of Archeology at Ankara, vols, XXII - XXIX, c/o The British Academy, Burlington House, Piccadilly, London, 1972 - 1979.

Angus, S., **The Environment of Early Christianity,** Scribner's Sons, New York, 1924.

Apocryphal New Testament, William Reeves, London, n.d.

Asch, Sholem, **The Apostle,** G.P. Putnam's Sons, New York, 1943.

Atlas of Ancient and Classical Geography, J. M. Dent & Sons Ltd., London, 1950.

Barclay, William, **Letters to the Seven Churches,** Abingdon Press, New York, 1958.

Barr, Stringfellow, **The Pilgrimage of Western Man,** Harcourt, Brace and Company, New York, 1949.

Baydur, Nezahat, **Kültepe (Kanesh) ve Kayseri Tarihi Üzerine Araştırmalar,** İstanbul Üniversitesi, Edebiyat Fakültesi Yayınları No. 1519; İstanbul, 1970.

Bean, George, E., **Aegean Turkey, An Archeological Guide,** Ernest Benn Limited, London, 1966.

————————**Lycian Turkey, An Archeological Guide,** Ernest Benn Limited, London, 1978.

———————— **Turkey Beyond the Meander, An Archeological Guide,** Ernest Benn Limited, London, 1971.

———————— **Turkey's Southern Shore, An Archeological Guide,** Ernest Benn Limited, London. 1968.

Berrett, LaMar C., **Discovering the World of the Bible,** Young House, Provo, Utah, 1973.

Bible Lands and the Cradle of Western Civilization (map), The National Geographic Society, Washington, 1946.

Bittel, Kurt, **Kleinasiatische Studien,** Adolf M. Hakkert, Amsterdam, 1967.

Boğazköy, Alacahöyük Tarihi Milli Park, Uzun Devreli Gelişme Planı, USAID Printing House, Sept. 1962.

Bossert, Helmuth, Th., **Altanatolien,** Ernest Wasmuth G.M.B.H., Berlin, 1942.

Boulanger, Robert, **Hachette World Guides Turkey,** Hachette, Paris, 1960, 1970.

Bridgewater and Sherwood, eds., **Columbia Encyclopedia,** Columbia University Press, New York, 1958.

Bucke, Emory, ed., **Interpreter's Dictionary of the Bible,** Abingdon Press, New York, 1962.

Buckmaster, Henrietta, **Paul, A Man Who Changed the World,** Mc Graw, New York, 1965.

BIBLICAL SITES IN TURKEY

Buttrick, George Arthur, commentary editor, **The Interpreter's Bible,** vols. 1-12, Abingdon-Cokesbury Press, Nashville, Tennessee, 1952.

Büyük Lûgat ve Ansiklopedi, cilt 1-12 ve ek, Meydan-Larousse, Meydan Yayınevi, İstanbul, 1969.

Campbell Angus S, ed., **Geology and History of Turkey,** Petroleum Exploration Society of Libya, Tripoli, Libya, 1971.

Campbell, Edward F., Jr. Freedman, David Noel, **The Biblical Archeologist Reader,** vol. III, Anchor Books, Doubleday & Company, Inc., Garden City, New York, 1970.

Clark, Francis E., **The Holy Land of Asia Minor,** Charles Scribner's Sons, New York, 1914.

Cornfield, Gaalyah, **Archeology of the Bible: Book by Book,** Harper & Row, Publishers, New York, 1976.

Cumont, Franz, **The Mysteries of Mithra,** Dover Publications, Inc., New York, 1956.

Darkot, Besim, Vistin and Bonapace, U., eds., **Modern Büyük Atlas,** Arkın Kitabevi, İstanbul, 1971.

Davies, A.P., **The First Christian,** The New American Library, a Mentor Book, New York, 1957.

Davison, Roderic H., **Turkey,** Prentice-Hall, Inc., New Jersey, 1968.

Deissmann, Adolf, **Paul, A Study in Social and Religious History,** Harper, New York, 1912, 1957.

De Planhol, X., ed., **Nagel's Encyclopedia-Guide Turkey,** Nagel Publishers, Geneva, 1968.

Der-Nersessian, Sirarpie and Vahramian, Herman, **Aght'amar,** Edizioni Ares, Milan, 1974.

Duran, Faik Sabri, **Büyük Atlas,** Viyana Coğrafya Enstitüsü, ed., Holzel, İstanbul, n.d.

Durant, Will, **The Story of Civilization,** Simon and Schuster, New York, 1935.

Edmonds, Anna G., **The Neolithic Revolution in Turkey,** Near East Mission, İstanbul, 1969.

Encyclopedia Britannica, Eleventh Edition, vols. 1-28, Encyclopedia Britannica, Inc., New York, 1911.

Encyclopedia Britannica, vols. 1-24, Encyclopedia Britannica, Inc. Chicago, 1966.

Flynn, Vernon, P. **The Seven Churches Today,** Amerikan Bord Neşriyat Dairesi, İstanbul, 1963.

Francis, Frank, ed., **Treasures of the British Museum,** Thames and Hudson, London, 1975.

Frazer, James George, **The Golden Bough,** abridged edition, Macmillan, London, 1971.

Friedrich, Johannes, **Kleinasiatische Sprachdenkmäler,** Walter de Gruyter & Co., Berlin, 1932.

Gelb, Ignace, J., **Hurrians and Subarians,** The Oriental Institute of the University of Chicago Studies in Ancient Oriental Civilization, No. 22, University of Chicago Press, Chicago, 1944.

Giovannini, Luciano, ed., **Arts of Cappadocia,** Barrie & Jenkins, London. 1971.

162

BIBLIOGRAPHY

Goguel, Maurice, **Jesus and the Origins of Christianity,** Harper, New York, 1932, 1960.

Good News for Modern Man, American Bible Society, New York, 1966.

Gordon, Cyrus H., **The Ancient Near East,** W.W. Norton & Company Inc., New York, 1965.

Gurney, O.R., **The Hittites,** Penguin Books, Middlesex, England, 1969. "The Sultantepe Tablets" in **Anatolia Studies, Journal of the British Institute of Archeology at Ankara,** vol. II, 1952. pp. 25-35.

Hamilton, Edith, **Mythology,** Little, Brown & Co., Boston, 1940.

Harrell, Betsy, **Mini Tours Book II,** Redhouse Press, İstanbul 1977.

Harrell, Betsy and Kalças, Evelyn Lyle, **Mini Tours Near İstanbul,** Redhouse Press, İstanbul, 1975.

Hastings, James, ed., **Dictionary of the Bible,** T.& T. Clark, Edinburg, 1929.

Herodotus, **The History of Herodotus,** George Rawlinson, trans., J.M. Dent & Sons Ltd., London, 1920.

Holy Bible, The, Authorized King James Version, Harper & Brothers, New York, n.d.

Interpreter's Bible, The, vols. 1-12, Abingdon-Cokesbury Press, New York, 1952.

Interpreter's Dictionary of the Bible, The, vols. 1-4, Abingdon Press, New York, 1962.

İslâm Ansiklopedisi, cilt 1-10, İstanbul Maarif Matbaası, İstanbul, 1940-1966.

James, E.O., **The Ancient Gods,** Weidenfeld and Nicolson, London, 1960.

Josephus, Flavius, **Complete Works of Flavius Josephus,** W. Whiston, trans., Armstrong and Berry, Baltimore, 1841.

Kelman, John and Fulleylove, John, **The Holy Land,** A. & C. Black Ltd. London, 1912.

Kinder, Hermann and Hilgemann, Werner, **The Penguin Atlas of World History,** vol. 1, Penguin Books, Middlesex, 1974.

Kinross, Lord, **Within the Tarsus,** Morrow, New York, 1955.

Lissner, Ivar, **The Living Past,** Penguin Books in association with Jonathan Cape, Middlesex, 1965.

Lloyd,Seton, **Early Highland Peoples of Anatolia,** Thames and Hudson, 1967.

Lloyd, Seton and Brice, William, "Harran" in **Anatolian Studies, Journal of the British Institute of Archeology at Ankara,** vol. I, 1951, pp. 77-111.

Lyle, Evelyn (Kalças), **The Search for the Royal Road,** Vision Press, London, 1966.

Mamboury, Ernest, **The Tourists' Istanbul,** Malcolm Burr, trans., Çituri Biraderler Basımevi, İstanbul 1953.

Mango, Andrew, **Discovering Turkey,** Hasting House, New York, 1971.

Mansel, Arif Müfid, **Silifke Kılavuzu,** Maarif Vekilliği Antikiteler ve Müzeler Direktörlüğü Anıtları Koruma Kurulu Seri I, sayı 8, Maarif Matbaası, İstanbul, 1943.

May, Herbert G., ed., **Oxford Bible Atlas,** Oxford University Press, London, 1962.

Meinardus, Otto F. A., **St. John of Patmos,** Lycabettus Press, Athens, 1974.

BIBLICAL SITES IN TURKEY

St. Paul in Ephesus, Lycabettus Press, Athens, 1973.

Mellaart, James, **Earliest Civilizations of the Near East,** Thames and Hudson, London, 1965.

Metzger, Henri, **Anatolia II,** Nagel Publishers, Geneva, 1969.

Les Routes de Saint Paul dans l'Orient Grec, Delachaux & Niestlé S. A., Neuchatel.

Moffratt, James, **An Introduction to the Literature of the New Testament,** Charles Scribner, New York, 1923.

Moorehead, Alan, **Gallipoli,** Harper, New York, 1956.

Morton, H.V., **In the Steps of St. Paul,** Dodd Mead & Co., New York, 1936.

Myers, F.W.H., **St.Paul,** Macmillan & Co., London, 1910.

Naim, Lâle, **Archeological Map of Western Anatolia,** n.p. or d.

Neill, Stephen, **Chrysostom and His Message,** Lutterworth Press, London, 1962.

New English Bible, second edition, Oxford and Cambridge University Presses, Oxford, 1970.

North, Martin, **The History of Israel,** 2nd edition, Harper & Row, Publishers, New York, 1960.

Otomobil ile Türkiye, The Shell Company of Turkey Ltd., İstanbul, n.d.

Peters, F.E., **The Harvest of Hellenism,** Simon and Schuster, New York, 1970.

Pettinato, Giovanni, **The Archives of Ebla,** Doubleday, New York, 1981.

Pritchard, James, B., ed., **Ancient Near Eastern Texts Relating to the New Testament,** Princeton University Press, Princeton, New Jersey, 1950.

Ramsay, William H., **St. Paul, the Traveller,** Hodder & Stoughton, London,

The Cities of St.Paul, Baker Book House, Grand Rapids, Michigan, 1963.

The First Christian Century, Hodder & Stoughton, London, 1897.

The Historical Geography of Asia Minor, vol. 4, Royal Geographical Society, John Murrey, London, 1890.

The Letters to the Seven Churches of Asia, Hodder & Stoughton, London, 1904.

Rice, D.S., "Studies in Medieval Harran, I" **Anatolian Studies, Journal of the British Institute of Archeology at Ankara,** vol. II, 1952, pp. 36-83.

Rogers, J.S., **In Search of St, Paul,** A. Barker, London. 1964.

Ropes, J. H., **The Apostolic Age,** Charles Scribner's Sons, New York, 1921.

Roux, Georges, **Ancient Iraq,** Penguin Books, Middlesex, 1964.

Segal, Judah Benzion, **Edessa and Harran,** School of Oriental and African Studies, University of London, 1963.

Edessa, "The Blessed City," Oxford University Press, 1970.

Shakespeare, William, **Anthony and Cleopatra,** in **The Complete Works of Shakespeare,** George Lyman Kittredge, ed., Ginn and Company, Boston, 1936.

Smith, William, **Smaller Classical Dictionary,** E.P. Dutton & Co., Inc., New York, 1958.

Stark, Freya, **Alexander's Parth,** Harcourt Brace, New York, 1958.

Ionia, John Murray, London, 1934.

The Lycian Shore, Harcourt Brace, New York, 1956.

BIBLIOGRAPHY

Stark, Freya and Roiter, Fulvio (photographer), **Turkey,** Thames and Hudson, London 1971.

Strabo, **The Geography of Strabo,** Hamilton & Falconer, trans., vols. 1-3, London, 1854.

Sumner-Boyd, Hilary and Freely, John, **Strolling Through Istanbul,** Redhouse Press, Istanbul, 1972.

Taşyürek, O. Altuğ, "Some New Assyrian Rock Reliefs in Turkey" in **Anatolian Studies,** vol. 25, 1975. pp. 169-176.

Villars, J.B., **T.E. Lawrence,** Sidgwick & Jackson, London, 1958.

Wiess, Johannes, **The Earliest Christianity,** Harper, 2 vols. New York, 1939.

Williams, Gwyn, **Eastern Turkey,** Faber and Faber, London, 1972.

Wilson, Charles William, **Handbook for Travellars in Asia Minor,** John Murray, London, 1895.

Wright, George Ernest and Filson, Lloyd Vivian, **The Westminster Historical Atlas to the Bible,** Westminster Press, Philadelphia, 1946.

Xenephon, **Anabasis, Books I-III, IV-VIII,** Carleton L. Brownson, trans., William Heinemann, London, 1921, 1922.

Yakar, Jak, "Hittite Involvement in Western Anatolia", in **Anatolian Studies,** vol, 26, 1976, p. 117-128.

Young, Robert, **Analytical Concordance to the Bible,** Funk & Wagnalls Company, New York, 1899.

LIST OF ILLUSTRATIONS

Cover picture: Marmaris harbor; photo by Ersin Alok

page 33:   Mt. Ararat (Büyük Ağrı Dağı); photo by Ticaret Matbaacılık   167
           T.A.Ş.
           Harran (Altınbaşak): town and fortress; photo by Ersin Alok

page 34:   Hattusas (Boğazkale): postern gate; photo by William A.
           Edmonds.

page 35:   Edessa (Urfa): Abd-er Rahman Mosque and pool of sacred
           carp; photo by William A. Edmonds

page 36:   Tigris (Dicle) River and Malabadi Bridge near Batman;
           photo by Ersin Alok
           Euphrates (Firat) River, Birecik; photo by Ersin Alok

page 37:   Göreme; photo by Ticaret Matbaacılık T.A.Ş.
           Gezer calendar in Archeological Museum, İstanbul;
           photo by Anna G. Edmonds

page 38:   Perga (Perge): portacoed street Of the agora; photo by
           Şadan Gökovalı
           Patara (Gelemis): theater and shifting sand; photo by
           Frederick D. Shepard

page 39:   Antioch of Pisidia (Yalvaç): frieze from temple; photo by
           Anna G. Edmonds
           Stone inscriptions from Lystra and Derbe in Konya
           Museum; photo by Anna G. Edmonds

page 40:   Miletus (Milet): theater: photo by Ticaret Matbaacılık T.A.Ş.

page 105: Tarsus: "St. Paul's Gate;" photo by Anna G. Edmonds
           Tarsus: Eski Cami; photo by William A. Edmonds.

page 106: Alexandria Troas: ruins of the Herodes Atticus Baths; photo
           by Anna G. Edmonds.
           Selçuk: baptistry of Church of St. John; photo by Ticaret
           Matbaacılık T.A.Ş.

page 107: Ephesus (Efes) : theater; photo by Ticaret Matbaacılık T.A.Ş.
           Second century A.D. statue of Artemis in Selçuk Museum;
           photo by Anna G. Edmonds

BIBLICAL SITES IN TURKEY

page 108: Ephesus (Efes): baptistry of Double Church; photo by Ticaret Matbaacılık T.A.Ş.
Meryem Ana: House of the Most Holy Virgin; photo by Ticaret Matbaacılık T.A.Ş.

page 109: Smyrna (İzmir): Roman Agora; photo by Ticaret Matbaacılık T.A.Ş.
Pergamum (Bergama): altar to Zeus; photo by Anna G. Edmonds

page 110: Thyatira (Akhisar): ruins of temple and colonnaded road; photo by Ticaret Matbaacılık T.A.Ş.
Sardis (Sart): façade of gymnasium; photo by William A. Edmonds

page 111: Sardis (Sart): temple to Artemis; photo by Ticaret Matbaacılık T.A.Ş.
Philadelphia (Alaşehir): wall and arch of Byzantine basilica; photo by William A. Edmonds

page 112: Laodicea (Laodikea): Nymphaeum or public fountain; photo by William A. Edmonds
Hierapolis (Pamukkale): Byzantine church; photo by William A. Edmonds.

Supplementary photographs by Sadık Oğuz:

1. Van Castle; 2. Ahtamar; 3. Trabzon: Church of St. Sophia; 4. Sumela: Monastery of the Virgin; 5. Antalya harbor; 6. Kaleköy near Kekova; 7. Fethiye: islands; 8. Myra: Church of St. Nicholas.

INDEX

A

Abd-er Rahman Medresesi 35, 41
Abel 10
Abgar 41
Abraham 9, 11, 17, 19, 31, 32, 51
Acts of Paul Thecia, The 76, 83
Adana 1, 28, 54
Adıyaman 50
Adramyttium 102
Aesop 136
Ahab 133
Ahimelech 19
Ahtamar 48
Ak Dağ 44
Akhisar 117, 131-133
Alaca Höyük 34, 43
Alashiya 24
Alaşehir 117, 137-139
Ala-ud-din Kaikubad I 90; II 6
Alexander the Great 6, 16, 45, 54, **69 ff.**, 90, 97, 102, 103, 115, 125-126,
128, 134
Alexandretta 54
Alexandria Troas 58, 82, 103-104, 106, 113
Altınbaşak 31-32, 33, 41
Alyattes 21, 23, 125
Amastris 59
Aastris 59
Amazons 59, 62, 125
Ambaris 25
Amisus 59
Amorites 14, 20, 24
Anabasis 79, 128
Anamites 14
Anaximander 97
Ancyra 56, 77, 80-81
Andrew 114
Andronicus 122

169

Anicetus 127
Anittas 44
Ankara 1, 5, 6, 56, 77, 80-81
Antalya 5, 54, 56, 89-90
Antigonus 103
Antioch of Pisidia 39, 56, 80, 81-83, 86, 91
Antioch on the Orontes 9, 54, 69-72, 74, 90, 91
Antiochus I 55; II 139; III the Great 53; father of Seleucus Nicator 69
Antipater Derbetes 87
Aphrodisias 16, 57, 62
Aphrodite 60, 62, 95, 96
Apollo 60, 62, 63, 93, 96, 98, 101, 126, 131, 133
Apollonia 80
Apollonius 91
Appius Claudius 139
Aquila 121, 122
Aram, Aramean, Aramaic 14, 15, 17, 20;
Arame 17
Aran's house 31
Ararat 26-27
Araxes River, Aras 1, 48, 50
Arcadian Way 120
Aristarchus 92
Aristotle 96, 102, 140
Arius 113
Arkites 14
Arphaxad 14, 15, 17
Artemis 60, 62, 90, 98, 101, 107, 119 ff., 134
Arvadites 14, 18
Asclepieum 65, 130; Asclepius 130
Ashkenaz 14, 22, 23
Ashurbanipal 16, 73, 134
Asia, Province of 6, 53, 57-58, 81, 98, 113, 114, 122, 123, 126, 128
Aspasia 97
Aspendos 54
Asshur (Noah's son) 14, 16; (War god) 30
Assos 58, 99, 102-103
Assuwa 18, 58
Assyria, Assyrians 5, 9, 16, 21-55 **passim**
Astarte 62
Aşıran Höyük 86-87
Athena 60, 63, 103, 129
Attalia 54, 89-90
Attalus I 81, 129; II 89, 137; III 128
Attis 61
Axylon 55

INDEX

Ayatekla 76
Ayio Theologo, Ayosoluk 123

B

Bafa Gölü 97
Balat 96-98
Ballıhisar 56, 81
Barak 41-42
Barnabas 70-92 **passim**
Basil 77-78, 144   171
Bathsheba 19
Baths of Faustina 97
Battle of Ipsus 69
Battle of Manzikert 6
Bayraklı 124
Behramköy 102-103
Bergama 58, 65, 128-131
Beth-togarmah 46
Beyşehir Gölü 1
Birecik, Birtha 41, 50
Bi'r Yakub 41
Bithynia, Bithyni 53, 59, 81, 103, 113, 114, 129
Bitlis 50
Bit Zamani 17
Boğazkale, Boğazköy 20, 43
Boz Dağı 133, 137
Bryges 57
Büyük Nefes Köy 79
Byzantium 6, 60, 114-116
Byzas 114

C

Caesar Augustus 56, 80, 85
Caesarea of Phoenicia 70, 102, 121
Caesarea Mazaca 42, 43, 55, 77-78
Cain 10
Caliph Omar 65
Calletebus 137
Calycadnus River 13, 54, 56, 76
Canaan, Canaanites 11, 12, 14, 18, 19-21, 32
Caphtorites 14, 19
Cappadocia 22, 23, 24, 43, 53, 55-56, 114
Carchemish 9, 19, 30, 32, 41-42
Caria, Carians 57, 62, 119

Carpus 104
Carrhae 32
Carura 140
Casluhites 14
Cassius 73
Cave of the Seven Sleepers 75-76
Cayster River 6, 119
Celâl-ed-din Rumî 84-85
Celtic tribes 22, 56, 79
Ceramic Gulf 57
Cestrus River 90, 91
Chalcedon 59, 114
Chaldea, Chaldini 26-27, 41
Chaldis 48
Chimera 89
Cicero 73, 79, 87, 139
Cilicia 17, 28, 53, 54, 56, 65, 71, 73, 74, 79
Cilician Gates 54
Cimmerii, Cimmarians 6, 21-27 **passim,** 45
Cizre 30
Claros 62, 126
Claudiopolis 54
Claudius 43, 121
Clazomene 99
Cleopatra 65, 73
Cnidus 57, 62, 92, 95-96
Coa 16, 26, 28
Colophon 99, 125
Colossae 57, 99-101
Commagene 50, 55
Constantine the Great 6, 113, 115
Constantinople 6, 72, 114-116
Cornelius 70
Cos, Gulf of 57
Cotyaeum 57
Crassus 32
Croesus 21, 23, 125, 134-136
Crusaders, Crusades 6, 31, 41, 71, 76, 80, 84, 126
Ctesias 95
Cudi Dağı 30-31
Cush 14, 18
Cyaxares 23
Cybele 45, 60, 61, 63, 81, 101, 134
Cydnus River 54, 73
Cyrus the Elder 6, 16, 23, 45, 135-136; the Younger 99
Cyzicus 58, 96, 97

INDEX

Ç

Çubuk Su 80

D

Danunas 54
Dardanii 60
Darius 23, 97, 114
Değle 86-87
Deiotarus 79
Demetrius 121-122
Demre 55, 92-93
Derbe 39, 77, 82, 86-87
Derinkuyu 79
Diana 62, 121-122
Dicle 1, 49-50
Didyma 62, 97-98
Diocletian 53, 92
Dionysus 60, 63, 96
Doğubayazıt 46, 48
Domitian 118
Dorylaeum 57
Double Church 108, 120, 124

E

Ea 47
Eber 13, 14
Ecumenical Councils: First 113; Second 115; Third 120; Fourth 114;
    Seventh 113-114
Eden 10, 51
Edessa 35, 41
Edremit 102
Eğridir Gölü 1
Elam 14
Elazığ 10
Elishah 14, 24
Epaphras 100, 101
Ephesus, Efes 53, 57, 62, 65, 86, 97 ff., 107, 108, 117, 118, 119-124,
    139
Ephron 19
Epictetus 102
Erythrea 99, 103
Esarhaddon 30
Esau 19, 41

Eshabikehf 75
Etruscan 25, 27
Eudoxus 95-96
Eumenes II 101, 137
Eunice 86
Euphrates River 1, 6, 16, 21, 32-47 **passim,** 36, 49-50, 51, 55, 139
Eusebius 41, 72, 127
Eutychus 104

F

Frederick Barbarossa 76
Fırat 1, 49-51

G

Gaius Julius Aquila 65
Gaius Julius Celsus Polemaeanus 66, 120
Gaius the Derbaean 87
Galatia, Galatians 22, 45, 53, 56, 74-91 **passim,** 114
Galen 130, 140
Gamaliel 74
Gamir 22
Gangra 59
Gauls 45, 56, 129
Gauraina 46
Gaziantep 50
Gelemiş 55, 93
Germaniceia 46
Gether 14
Gevaş 48
Gezer calendar 37, 115, 116
Gilgamesh Epic 42, 43, 47
Gilistra 85-86
Girgashites 14
Gog 23
Gomer 14, 22, 23
Goncalı 117
Gordium 21, 25, 30, 45
Gordius 57
Göreme 37, 78
Greene, Olive 99
Gürün 13, 22, 46
Gyges, Gugu 16, 134

H

Hadrian 93, 120
Halicarnassus 57, 125
Halys 1
Ham, Hamitic, Hamites 12, 13, 14, 18-21
Hamathites 14
Handbook for Travellers in Asia Minor 99
Hannibal 81
Harran 9, 11, 17, 19, 29, 31-41, 33
Hattusas 19, 34, 42, 43, 44
Havilah 14
Hazar, Lake 10, 50
Helen 102
Heraclea Perinthus 60
Heracleia 97
Hermias 102
Hermus River (Gediz) 131, 138; (Meriç) 60
Herodes Atticus Bath 103
Herodotus 21, 25, 57, 58, 99, 125, 134, 136
Hesiod 60, 120
Heth 14, 18, 19-20
Hezekiah 9, 17, 115-116
Hierapolis 100, 101-102, 112, 140
Hittite, Hittites 5, 9, 15-86 **passim,** 125
Hivites, Horites 14, 18, 20-21
Homer 21, 58, 59, 60, 63, 93, 120, 125
Hsiung-Nu 27
Hul 14
Hurrian, Hurri 16, 18, 20-21, 24, 41, 43
Hyroeades 135

I

İconium 76, 77, 83-85, 86, 90
Ignatius 72, 100, 127
Ilistra 85-86
Ilium 58
Ionia, Ionians 6, 23, 125, 134
Isaac 13, 19, 32, 51
Isauria 56
Ishmael 51
Ishtar 62
Isij 58
İspuinis 48

İ

İskenderun 50, 54, 72
İstanbul 1, 60, 114-116
İzmir 1, 16, 58, 124-128
İzmit 59, 113
İznik 59, 113-114

J

176

Jacob 13, 19, 32, 41
James 71
Japheth, Japhetic, Japhathites 12, 13, 14, 21-26
Javan 14, 23-24
Jebusites 14, 20
Jezebel 133
John 118-144 **passim**
John Mark 89, 91
Josephus 25, 42, 47, 116, 132
Josiah 42
Judah 13, 44
Judas 71
Julius 92, 102
Julius Caesar 32, 73, 79
Junias 122
Justinian 80, 123

K

Kale 50
Kanesh 16, 19, 30, 43-44
Karababa 50
Karabel 18
Karabur 30-31
Karalis Lake 56
Karasu 50
Kaymaklı 79
Kayseri 1, 16, 19, 24, 55, 77-78, 81
Kerti Höyük 86-87
Kittim 14, 24
Kizzuwatna 28, 73
Knidos 95-96
Konya 1, 5, 56, 83-85
Kubaba 61
Kültepe 16, 30, 43-44

INDEX

L

Laban 41
Lade 97
Laodicea, Laodikea 57, 100, 112, 117, 118, 139-141
Larbanas 86
Lebedus 99
Lehabites 14
Leleges 124
Limnai Lake 56
Lucian 55
Lud 14, 16, 23, 42
Luke 92, 98, 104, 121
Luqqa 55
Lusna 86
Luwites 43
Lycaonia 56, 85
Lycia, Lycians 55, 92-93
Lycus River (Çuruksu) 140; (Kum Çayı) 131
Lydia, Lydians 6, 14, 16, 18-28 **passim**, 45-49, 58, 63, 65, 102, 119, 131, 134-137, 138
Lydia of Thyatira 132-133
Lydus 58
Lygus 114
Lysimachia 72
Lysimachus 103, 128, 131
Lystra 39, 77, 83, 85-86

M

Madai 14, 22, 23
Magna Mater Magnum Idaea 81
Magnesia on the Meander 53, 57, 82
Magog 14, 23
Makhramion 102
Manneans 27
Marco Polo 47
Marcus Aurelius 126
Marcus Aurelius Caracalla 32
Mardin 50
Mark Anthony 65, 73
Marmara Ereğlisi 60
Marsyas 63
Mary 123-124
Mash 14
Mausolus 57

Meander River 1, 63, 97, 138
Medes 22, 23, 26
Mehmet II 6, 115
Meles 126
Men 80, 82, 101, 140
Menuas 49
Meremlik 76
Meriç 60
Merodach-baladan 26
Meryem Ana 108, 124
Meshech 14, 16, 21-26, 42, 44-45, 55
Mesopotamia 16, 50
Mevlevi Dervişler 84-85
Midas, Mita 16, 21, 25, 45, 57, 63
Miletus, Milet 40, 57, 58, 75, 96-98, 125
Minni 22, 26, 27, 55
Mithra 60, 61-62, 89
Mitanni 16, 21
Mizraim 14, 16, 18-19
Mt. Ararat 1, 26, 30, 33, 46-48
Mt. Argaeus 56
Mt. Cadmus 100
Mt. Ida 58, 102
Mt. Mycale 99
Mt. Olympus 59
Mt. Nimrud 55
Mt. Pagus 125
Mt. Pieria 72
Mt. Pion 120
Mt. Tmolus 133-134, 137
Murat 50
Murtuna 90-92
Mushki (See Meshech)
Mustafa Kemal Atatürk 2, 4-5, 81
Mycale 63
Myra 55, 90, 92-93, 96, 102
Mysia 58, 104
Mysus 58
Myus 99

N

Nahor 17
Naphtuhites 14
Nebuchadrezzar 23, 42
Necho 42

INDEX

Nefertiti 19
Nemesis 125
Nemrut Dağı 55
Nero 75, 96
Nesa 44
Nevşehir 79
Nicaea 6, 59, 113-114
Nicholas of Antioch 69
Nicolatians 124, 130
Nicomedia 59, 113
Nimrod 14
Noah 9, 12, 13-26, 30, 42, 47, 75
Nuzi 20

O

Odun İskelesi 103-113
Olympus 89
Omayyads 31
Onesimus 100-101
Orham 41
Ormuzd 61
Orontes River 13, 16, 69, 71, 72
Orpheus 60
Orrhoe, Orhai, Osrhoene 41

P

Pactolus River 134
Padan Aram 17
Pamphylia 54
Pamukkale 101-102
Pan 60, 63
Pànayır Dağı 120
Panionia, Pan Ionic 63, 99
Paphlagonia 22, 59
Papias 101
Paris 102
Parthians 32
Patara 38, 55, 62, 93
Pathrusites 14
Paul 9, 52, 56, 64-144 **passim**
Pausanias 60
Pelopia 131
Perga, Perge 38, 54, 82, 90-92, 139
Pergamum, Pergamenes 58, 65, 81, 101, 102, 109, 117, 126, 128-131, 137

Pericles 97
Pessinus 56, 77, 81
Peter 70, 71, 114
Philadelphia 111, 117, 118, 137-139, 143
Philemon 100
Philip 101
Philip of Macedon 72, 102, 114
Philistines 14, 18
Phocaea 99
Phoenicia, Phoenicians 17, 19
Phrygia, Phrygians 6, 21, 27, 45, 57, 61-82 **passim,** 97, 138, 140
Pisidia 56
Plancia Magna 91
Plato 96, 102
Pliny the Elder 99; the Younger 119, 131
Plutarch 32, 89
Pluto, Plutonium 101
Polycarp 72, 126-127, 144
Pompeiopolis 76
Pompey 32, 76, 89
Pontus 53, 59, 114, 121
Pope Adrian I 114
Pope John Paul II 124
Pope Paul VI 124
Poseidon 60, 63, 96, 99, 101, 103
Praxiteles 95
Priene 57, 97, 99
Priscilla, Prisca 121, 122
Prusa 59
Ptolemy 65, 72
Purple dye 11, 18, 24, 132
Put 14, 18, 23
Pylaemenes 59
Pyramus 1
Pythias 102

Q

Qadesh 116

R

Raamah 14
Rachel 41
Ramsay, William 66-67, 138, 140
Ramses III 25

Rebecca 19, 41
Red Court, Red Basilica 130
Riphath 14, 22
Rodanim 14, 24
Romanus IV Diogenes 6
Rosh 23
Royal Road 28, 44, 50, 81, 136, 138
Rusa I 21, 25, 49; III 49
Ruth 51

S

Sabtah 14
Sabtecha 14
Sagalassus 56
St. Jerome 71
St. John the Apostle 123, 130
St. John Chrysostom 72
St. Mary of the Armenians 80
St. Nicholas 90, 92-93
St. Paul's Gate 75, 105
St. Paul's Prison 123
St. Peter's Grotto 71
St. Sophia (Constantinople) 115; (Nicaea) 113-114
St. Thecla 76, 83
Sam'al 17
Samandağ 72
Samosata, Samsat 50
Sangarius River 1, 44, 57, 81
Saracens 92
Sarah 19, 31
Sardis, Sart 6, 16, 18, 23, 28, 49, 50, 58, 64, 99, 110, 111, 118, 125, 131,
     133-137, 138, 139
Sarduri I 26; III 26
Sargon II 9, 19, 25, 26, 28, 42, 55
Sarus 1
Sayings of Jesus 101
Scythians 22, 23, 26
Sea People 18, 24, 25
Seba 14
Sebasteia 46, 59
Selçuk 106, 119, 123
Seleucia of Isauria 13, 54, 76
Seleucia Pieria 13, 54, 72
Seleucids 6, 50, 53, 55, 65, 72, 74, 131
Seleucus Nicator 69, 72, 81, 131, 132

Selinus River 130
Semitic, Semites 12, 14, 15-17
Sennacherib 9, 17, 25, 27, 30, 73
Sepharad 26, 27-28, 49
Septimius Severus 114
Serapis 120, 130
Sergius Paulus 91
Seth 75
Shamash 30
Shelah 14
Shem 12, 13, 14, 15-17
Side 54, 89
Sidon 14, 18
Silas 71, 91
Siirt 50
Silifke 76
Siloam inscription 115-116
Simeon Stylites 71
Sin 30, 31, 32
Sinites 14
Sinope, Sinop 59, 97
Smyrna 58, 109, 117, 118, 124-128, 143
Socrates 97
Soli 76
Solomon 20, 115
Solon 134-135
Sostratus 95
Southeastern Anatolia Project 50
Statius Quadratus 127
Stephen 69, 74
Strabo 59, 65, 103, 125, 140
Süleyman the Magnificent 6
Süleyman Şah 6
Suppiluliumas 5, 19, 28

T

Tabal 24, 25
Table of Nations 13-26
Tahtalı Dağı 46
Tamar 44
Tamerlane 6
Tarshish 14, 23, 24
Tarsus 9, 24, 64, 65, 71, 73-76, 105
Tartessus 24
Tarz 73

INDEX

Tatian 41
Tavium 56, 77, 79, 81
Tectosages 56, 79
Tell Tainat 16
Tellus of Athens 135
Telmessus 55
Teos 99
Terah 17, 32
Terizzites 20
Termessus 56
Thales 97
Theodosius I 115
Thiras, Thirasians 26
Thrace, Thracians 23, 26, 59-60
Thutmose III 21
Thyatira 111, 117, 118, 131-133
Tiberius 43
Tiglath-pileser I 25, III 9, 16, 26
Tigranes the Great 48
Tigris River 1, 11-17 **passim,** 30, 36, 49-50, 51
Timothy 86, 103
Tiras 14, 26
Titus 104
Togarmah, Tegarama, Tilgarimmu 13, 14, 22, 23, 46
Tolistobogii 56, 79
Toprakkale 26, 48-49
Trajanopolis 57
Trapezus, Trabzon 27, 59
Troas, Troad 58, 103-113, 106
Trocmi 56, 79
Trogillium 99
Tropium 95
Troy, Trojans 58; Trojan War 60, 93
Tubal 14, 21-26 **passim,** 42-43, 45
Tushpa 26, 48
Tyana 19
Tyrannus 120, 121
Tuz gölü 1, 55

U

Ugarit 24
Uluborlu 80
Unu Höyük 86-87
Urartu, Urartian 6, 9, 21-25 **passim,** 26-27, 46-48, 55
Urfa 21, 41, 50

Ur of the Chaldees 17, 32
Uriah 19
Utnapishtim 47
Uz 14

Ü

Ürgüp 78

V

Van, Van Lake 1, 26, 27, 48-49

W

Wilson, Charles 99

X

Xanthus 55, 93
Xenephon 79, 128
Xenocrates 102
Xerxes 99

Y

Yalvaç 56, 80, 81-83
Yazılı Kaya 25, 43

Z

Zemarites 14, 18
Zeus 16, 60, 63-64, 85, 129, 130, 133, 140
Zoroaster 56